Includes Consecration
to St. Joseph by
Fr. Michael Gaitley, MIC

MEET
YOUR
SPIRITUAL FATHER

A BRIEF INTRODUCTION TO ST. JOSEPH

MEET YOUR SPIRITUAL FATHER

A BRIEF INTRODUCTION TO ST. JOSEPH

DR. MARK MIRAVALLE

LIGHTHOUSE CATHOLIC MEDIA + MARIAN PRESS

2015

Available from either of the following:

Lighthouse Catholic Media, NFP
303 E. State Street
Sycamore, IL 60178

Phone: 866-767-3155
www.lighthousecatholicmedia.org

Marian Helpers Center
Stockbridge, MA 01263

Prayerline: 800-804-3823
Orderline: 800-462-7426
www.marian.org

ISBN: 978-1-59614-314-2
Library of Congress Catalog Number: 2014921528

Cover Design: Devin Schadt

Page Layout: Kathy Szpak

Editing and Proofreading: Fr. Michael Gaitley, MIC, David Came,
Andrew Leeco, and Chris Sparks.

Imprimi Potest:
Very Rev. Kazimierz Chwalek, MIC
Provincial Superior
The Blessed Virgin Mary, Mother of Mercy Province
Congregation of Marian Fathers of the Immaculate Conception of the B.V.M.
December 12, 2014
Feast of Our Lady of Guadalupe

Printed in the United States of America

Dedicated
to Joseph, my son

Contents

Introduction

My prayer for you as you read this book is that you will get to meet your spiritual father, St. Joseph. Or, if you've already met him, I pray that you will grow more deeply in love with him — a love that should rank among your devotion to the saints right after your unique love for your spiritual mother, Mary.[1]

You may be familiar with another book I wrote called *Meet Your Mother*. In that book, my goal was to introduce people to our heavenly mother, Mary, in a simple, easy-to-read way. This book is like that one in that it is a relatively simple, easy-to-read introduction to St. Joseph. However, this book will also go a bit more deeply into the theology of St. Joseph. I've chosen to add more theology because, quite frankly, there just aren't a lot of resources that give answers to the important questions about St. Joseph, and answering such questions requires some research and study.

What kinds of questions am I talking about? Well, for instance, it's hard to find answers to questions about St. Joseph's "doubt," his virginity, his age, and whether or not we can call him the "father" of Jesus in any sense. Getting such answers will help us to better understand and appreciate our spiritual father.

How do I propose to approach these questions? In other words, what's the itinerary for this Josephite journey?

Well, we're going to begin with the inspired revelation of St. Joseph as it is found in the Old and New Testaments of the Bible. As we travel through the biblical events concerning this man who was so close to Jesus and Mary, we'll stop to discuss the major questions and issues that arise from the biblical texts — like the ones I just mentioned. As the questions come up in our biblical journey, we'll deal with each one of them in turn.

After the biblical treatment of St. Joseph, we'll take a look at how the early Church understood him, the development of devotion to St. Joseph during the Middle Ages, and then proceed on to the modern period with its emphasis on papal tributes and Marian apparitions. Finally, we'll talk about St. Joseph and *you* — the major forms of devotion by which you can grow closer to our great saint, leading up to the pinnacle of Josephite love: a personal consecration to our spiritual father.

Before we begin looking at St. Joseph in Sacred Scripture, I think it will first be helpful to hear some testimonies to the greatness of St. Joseph that come from various saints and popes. As you read those testimonies and journey through this book, I encourage you to keep one simple guiding principle ever in your mind and heart: *Who St. Joseph was to Jesus, St. Joseph is to you.* In other words, as St. Joseph was a virginal father to Jesus, the Head of the Body of Christ, so also is he a father to you, to each and every member of Christ's Body, and to any human being who opens his or her heart to his spiritual fatherhood. Simply put, you could have the same human spiritual father that Jesus Christ had while on earth, if you allow St. Joseph into your heart as Jesus did — if you allow yourself to truly meet your spiritual father.

Chapter 1

Testimonies to St. Joseph's Greatness

How great is St. Joseph? How powerful is his intercession? How important is it that we turn to him with our prayers? Let's listen to some testimonies from saints, popes, and miserable me.

First, we have the testimony of the Catholic Church's "Doctor of Prayer," St. Teresa of Avila, regarding "the glorious St. Joseph":

> I wish I could persuade everyone to be devoted to the glorious St Joseph, for I have great experience of the blessings which he can obtain from God. I do not remember that I have ever asked anything of him which he has failed to grant. I am astonished at the great favors which God has bestowed on me through this blessed saint, and at the perils from which he has delivered me, both in body and in soul.
>
> To other saints, the Lord seems to have given grace to help us in some of our necessities. But my experience is that St Joseph helps us in them all; also that the Lord wishes to teach us that, as He was Himself subject on earth to St. Joseph, so in Heaven He now does all that Joseph asks. This has also been

the experience of other persons whom I have advised
to commend themselves to the saint. ...

I only request, for the love of God, whoever will
not believe me will test the truth of what I say, for
he will see by experience how great a blessing it is to
recommend oneself to this glorious patriarch and to
be devoted to him.[2]

Now that's one amazing testimony! I'm particularly
moved by that last line, the challenge St. Teresa puts to us
"to test the truth" of what she says. I affirm with this great
mystic and Doctor of the Church that anyone who turns to
St. Joseph will not be disappointed.

Other Doctors of the Church point to St. Joseph's
greatness. For example, St. Francis de Sales highlights his
almost unsurpassed holiness: "Although it is true that
Mary possessed every virtue in a higher degree than is
attainable by any other pure creature, yet it is quite certain
that the glorious St. Joseph was the being that approached
most nearly to that perfection."[3]

Also, so many popes have happily thrown in
their own sublime praise of the "Just Man" of the New
Testament. Blessed Pius IX declared him the "Patron of
the Universal Church,"[4] which is a title above and beyond
that given to any other saint in history, except for Mary.
Leo XIII confirms of St. Joseph that "there is no doubt he
approached nearer than any other to that superabundant
dignity of hers."[5] Pius XI even speaks of his "all-powerful
intercession" (through his relationship to Jesus and Mary)
as the true Head of the Holy Family:

As St. Joseph was truly the head or the master of
that house [Nazareth], his intercession cannot be

but all-powerful. For what could Jesus and Mary refuse to St. Joseph, as he was entirely devoted to them all his life, and to whom they truly owed the means of their earthly existence?"[6]

The papal superlatives go on and on. (Indulge me as I mention a few more.) Saint John XXIII declared St. Joseph the Patron of the Second Vatican Council and inserted his name into the Roman Canon of the Mass.[7] And more recently, St. John Paul II confirmed the unique sanctity and dignity of St. Joseph in his Apostolic Letter *Redemptoris Custos* (*Guardian of the Redeemer*), where he identifies him as "the Just Man," a "perfection of charity" that leads to a harmonious blending of contemplation and action: "In Joseph, the apparent tension between the active and the contemplative life finds an ideal harmony that is only possible for those who possess the perfection of charity."[8]

Since his election in 2013, Pope Francis has wasted no time in giving historic honor to St. Joseph. In one of his first acts as Holy Father, he decreed that the name of St. Joseph was to be inserted after the reference to the Virgin Mary in all four of the main Eucharistic Prayers.[9] Pope Francis's strong personal love for St. Joseph is likewise indicated by the saint's presence on his papal coat of arms in the form of a vine.[10]

Farther, it's significant that the Pope turns to St. Joseph frequently throughout his day and entrusts various intentions to him. He takes the saint's role as Patron of the Universal Church to heart and puts him to work. How does he do it?

On May 1, 2014, the *Vatican Insider* reported that Pope Francis had placed a statuette of St. Joseph outside the door of his room in St. Martha's House where he presently resides. The Holy Father routinely places special petitions that he entrusts to St. Joseph, written on small scraps of paper, under the statuette. As the Swiss guards in attendance confirmed:

> Francis has a great devotion for St. Joseph and even keeps a statuette of the saint in a marble-topped dark wooden chest of drawers just outside his room (Room 201) in St. Martha's House. The Pope slips prayer requests he has written under the pedestal and the pieces of paper grow in number — "the Holy Father really makes the saint work."[11]

Even the Mother of God offers testimony to the holiness of her husband and how it's imperative for the human family, in our present situation, to show proper honor to this greatest male saint. For example, during the Marian apparitions at Fatima when 70,000 people witnessed the historic "solar miracle" on October 13, 1917, St. Joseph appeared with the Child Jesus and blessed the world as a sign of the importance of devotion to St. Joseph for the "Triumph of the Immaculate Heart," promised by Our Lady of Fatima.[12] Also, during the more recently reported revelations of Our Lady of America (revelations strongly supported by Cardinal Raymond Burke and worthy of our consideration as well), the Blessed Virgin refers to the holiness of St. Joseph as the fruit of his constant awareness of the indwelling Trinity. At the same apparition, St. Joseph himself speaks of his unique God-given privileges of grace and calls for a new devotion to his "Pure Heart" as well as to his "Fatherhood."[13]

Lastly, and by far the least impressively, I want to offer my own humble testimony of gratitude to the magnificently powerful intercession of St. Joseph. At the greatest times and also the most trying times of my life, St. Joseph has been there as the "Mirror of Patience," the "Terror of Demons," and the "Glory of Home Life," making up for my failings through his most generous and powerful intercession. From guiding my doctoral dissertation, to finding our family home, to assisting in so many times of domestic need, St. Joseph has always, always been there. For me, he is not only the holiest human after his wife but also an all-enduring, never tiring, forever-loving spiritual father and friend. For this, I could never offer him proper thanks and praise.

St. Joseph in the Old Testament

Saint Joseph in the Old Testament? But he's a New Testament figure! True. But the Old Testament *foreshadows* the New Testament. In other words, God gives us hints of his big revelations coming up in the New Testament by offering clues in the Old Testament. These clues are called "types." More specifically, a "type" is a person, place, thing, or event that refers to something beyond itself — something more important than itself.

The Two Josephs

Amidst the many types of St. Joseph found in the Old Testament, especially among the great patriarchs and kings such as Abraham, Isaac, Jacob, Moses, David, and numerous others, there's one extremely important human type regarding St. Joseph. His name is — you guessed it — *Joseph.*

The Old Testament Joseph was, as most of us know, one of the twelve sons of Jacob, whom God named Israel. He was sold into slavery by his envious brothers and through the extraordinary Providence of God, was eventually placed at the right hand of the Egyptian Pharaoh in a position of great power and intercession.

17

Through his manifest wisdom and prophetic dreams, Joseph won the confidence of the Egyptian ruler. Joseph's dreams about the upcoming famines directed the Pharaoh to plan ahead for these future scarcities by stockpiling huge quantities of grain in order to survive the coming food shortage. Joseph was then given the task of overseeing the process of preparation for the famine, an enormously important task upon which the lives of everyone in the kingdom, including the Pharaoh and his royal family, depended. The Egyptian ruler further placed Joseph in charge of the prudent distribution of the food supply, and once the famine approached, he directed the people of Egypt with these profound and prophetic words, "Go to Joseph" (Gen 41:55).

Eventually, Joseph became an instrument of temporal salvation for the Egyptian Kingdom and for his own People of Israel. He likewise intercedes to bring forth a family reconciliation that eventually leads to the reunification of the future leaders of the twelve tribes under their father, Jacob or "Israel."[14]

Now let's look at some of the rather remarkable similarities between the Old Testament Joseph and the New Testament St. Joseph:

1. Both had fathers named "Jacob."
2. Both received critically important messages from God through dreams.
3. Both experienced unexpected trips to Egypt.
4. Both had vocational calls that formed them as models of chastity (St. Joseph in remaining a virgin in his marriage to Mary and the Old Testament Joseph in rebuffing the advances of Potiphar's wife).
5. Both were in the lineage of the great Patriarchs of Israel.

These similarities are why saints and scholars see in the Old Testament Joseph such a clear type of the New Testament Joseph. As the first Joseph became an instrument of earthly salvation and protection for Jacob and the descendants of Israel through his constant fidelity to God under the greatest of trials, so, too, does St. Joseph, through his cooperation with God under the greatest of trials as Guardian of the Redeemer, become a fatherly instrument of protection for the Savior of the world. As such, he is an instrument for bringing the entire world spiritual protection and salvation through Jesus. Further, notice how, with both Josephs, we have a persevering and faithful father figure who saves his loved ones from death, whether the threat comes from famine in the land or from the murderous designs of a tyrant like King Herod. So as members of God's family today, which is the Church, we can reflect on how the Patriarch Joseph in his saving role for Israel helps us better appreciate St. Joseph in his role as the protector and guardian of not only Jesus but of each of us. Thus, the Patriarch Joseph illumines for us the powerful role of glorious St. Joseph as our spiritual father and even paves the way for him being recognized as Patron of the Universal Church.

There's one other thing about the Old Testament Joseph that may shed light on St. Joseph in the New Testament.

St. Joseph's Assumption?

Some Doctors of the Church and other ecclesiastical writers see a clue about a possible resurrection and assumption of St. Joseph (not a Church doctrine, but an acceptable theological opinion) indicated by the way the bodily remains of the Old Testament Joseph were returned to Israel at the time of the Exodus.

When the People of Israel departed on their historic return to the Promised Land of Israel, they carried the "bones of Joseph" with them into the Promised Land, as Joseph himself foretold: "Then Joseph took an oath of the sons of Israel, saying, 'God will visit you, and you shall carry up my bones from here'" (Gen 50:25; see also Ex 13:19). In light of this, it is possible that St. Joseph, because of his union with Jesus and Mary, would be the first, after the resurrection of Jesus, to be brought body and soul into the eternal "promised land" of heaven (see Mt 27:52).

Several great Josephite theologians such as St. Francis de Sales, St. Bernadine of Siena, Francisco Suarez, and others taught that while an early, bodily resurrection and assumption of St. Joseph is not a doctrine of the Church, it is still an acceptable theological opinion.[15] Interestingly, St. Pope John XXIII refers to the Assumption of St. Joseph as an acceptable pious belief in a 1960 Homily on the Ascension of Jesus.[16]

It seems appropriate that if any saint would experience an early assumption of his body, it would be the virginal father of the Savior and spouse to the Immaculate One (not in virtue of an immaculate conception, as was uniquely the case with Our Lady, but due to his interior unity with Jesus and Mary and his pre-eminent sanctity after Mary).

St. Joseph's Old Testament Family Line

Have you ever been to Mass and listened to the proclamation of the Gospel that goes on and on about how so-and-so became the father of so-and-so and then so-and-so became the father of so-and-so, and on and on? During that reading, which I myself have proclaimed as a deacon, people begin to get a glazed look in their eyes, like they're ready to fall asleep. But we shouldn't fall asleep! The Old Testament lineage (family line of descent) of St. Joseph (and ultimately of Jesus) is very important.

Why? Why is it so important? It's because the lineage of St. Joseph is what established Jesus as the fulfillment of the Old Testament prophecies that the Savior would come from the "House of David." For instance, we read in Isaiah:

> For to us a child is born, to us a son is given; and the government will be upon his shoulder, and his name will be called "Wonderful Counselor, Mighty God, Everlasting Father, Prince of Peace." Of the increase of his government and of peace there will be no end, upon the throne of David, and over his kingdom, to establish it, and to uphold it with justice and with righteousness from this time forth and for evermore. The zeal of the LORD of hosts will do this (Is 9:6-7).

It's thanks to Joseph's fatherhood of Jesus that our Savior has the right to be called a descendant of David in the line of the Patriarchs! But why is this the case? It's because a proper Jewish genealogy must trace the male line of descent. That's why when we hear that long Gospel passage of Jesus' genealogy, it always repeats that so-and-so became the *father* of so-and-so. Thus, it truly is from *St. Joseph* and not from Mary that Jesus will receive his lineage of royal, Davidic blood.

Let's look more closely at that passage with all the so-and-sos.

It comes from the Gospel of Matthew, right at the very beginning. Because it comes at the beginning, Matthew means to highlight the Old Testament lineage of St. Joseph as particularly important. Why does he do this? Precisely to make clear to all readers that Jesus is the Messiah who has descended, as was foretold, from the royal lineage of David.

Now, as we will discuss later (in chapter six), even though St. Joseph is not the biological father of Jesus, he remains the true virginal and "moral" father of Jesus, and hence the true legal father of the Savior.

The Fatherhood of St. Joseph

What we also see foreshadowed in the Old Testament is the "fatherhood" of St. Joseph, which will, in turn, be the ultimate symbol-in-action of the very Fatherhood of God.

In diverse but complementary ways, all the Patriarchs of the Old Testament — from Abraham, to Moses, to David — reveal the infinite Paternity of the Heavenly Father. Whether it be, for example, in Abraham's sacrificial fatherhood in faith and perfect fidelity and obedience to God, or in Moses' ultra-courageous guiding, protecting, enduring, and saving of the Chosen People during the Exodus, or in David's paternal shepherding of Kingdom of Israel, each patriarch in his own way manifests one glimmering side of the divine gem that is the inestimable loving and providing Fatherhood of Abba, Father of all Mankind.[17]

No single human who has ever lived comprises a better "icon" of the perfect Fatherhood of God than the husband of Mary and virginal father of Jesus: St. Joseph. Whatever aspect of true and holy fatherhood that is revealed to us in part through Old Testament patriarchs and kings is revealed to us in a *greater, more complete, and fully integrated way* in the Just Man of Nazareth. As we shall see, God the Father placed his greatest paternal virtues in the man who would be "father" to God's divine Son while he was on earth.

Simply put: *The Fatherhood of God, which is revealed partially in the Old Testament patriarchs, prophets, and kings, is now revealed in its greatest and most complete human expression in the person of St. Joseph.* And as we've learned in this chapter, the richness of who St. Joseph is is not limited to his appearances in the New Testament. Rather, the Old Testament foreshadows St. Joseph's greatness precisely in the Old Testament types, of which the most important one is Joseph the Patriarch. He was the one Pharaoh instructed his people to implore in their need, telling them, "Go to Joseph." Yes, let's go to Joseph, who, as we'll learn in the next chapter, is more than just the "just man" of the New Testament.

Chapter 3

More Than Just a 'Just Man'

"The only thing the New Testament says about St. Joseph is simply that he was a 'just man.'" Is this frequently quipped comment about St. Joseph true or false? The New Testament does, in fact, call St. Joseph a "just man" — so that's true. But is this the only thing the New Testament says about St. Joseph? Definitely *not*. There is *much, much more* revealed about who this "just man" is and what he does in the sacred pages of the Gospels.

Let's start by just listing the major New Testament references to our great saint:

1. The genealogy of Jesus (Mt 1:1-16; Lk 3:23-38).
2. The betrothal (first part of marriage) of St. Joseph to the Virgin Mary (Mt 1:18-19; Lk 1:27).
3. The "Just Man" reference (Mt 1:19).
4. The Angel's revelation to St. Joseph in a dream regarding Mary's virginal conception of Jesus (Mt 1:20-23).
5. The second part (solemnization) of his marriage to the Virgin Mary (Mt 1:24-25).
6. The journey to Bethlehem (Lk 2:1-7).
7. The adoration of the shepherds in St. Joseph's presence (Lk 2:16).

25

8. Saint Joseph naming the Baby Jesus (Mt 1:25; Lk 2:21).
9. Saint Joseph's role in the Presentation of the Infant Jesus in the temple (Lk 2:22-36).
10. The Angel instructing St. Joseph to flee to Egypt with the Child and his mother (Mt 2:13-15).
11. The Angel's instruction to St. Joseph to return to Israel (Mt 2:19-23).
12. Saint Joseph's life at Nazareth with Jesus and Mary (Mt 2:23; Lk 2:39).
13. Saint Joseph's part in the losing and finding of the Christ Child in the temple (Lk 2:41-50).

Now that's a lot of biblical revelation to unravel and appreciate. While we'll be referring back to these New Testament passages throughout this concise work, let's begin with some of the first Gospel revelations about St. Joseph: his betrothal and marriage to Mary and what historically has been referred to as the "doubt" of St. Joseph.

The Betrothal and Marriage of Joseph and Mary

To understand properly what the Gospels say about the betrothal and marriage of St. Joseph and the Virgin, we have to do a little historical and theological digging into the Jewish understanding of these two realities at the time of Jesus. Now, bear with me. While what follows certainly goes into a bit more detail than what you'll find elsewhere in this concise guide to the saint, it's the best and clearest way I know of to clear up any confusion regarding the betrothal and marriage of Joseph and Mary.

During biblical times, the idea of "betrothal" in Jewish law and custom meant something much more than our contemporary concept of engagement. Betrothal was actually "part one" of marriage. In other words, betrothal began the marriage. Then, the bride was typically brought into the home of her husband several months or even a year later. Normally, the wife did not enter her husband's home until "part two" (or the "solemnization") of the marriage took place. As the *Jewish Encyclopedia* explains:

> The root, to betroth ... must be taken in this sense, that is, to contract an actual, though incomplete marriage ... the rabbinical law declares that the betrothal is equivalent to an actual marriage, and only to be dissolved by an actual divorce.[19]

A modern historian of 1st century Jewish history further explains the role of betrothal in a traditional Jewish marriage:

> Betrothal was a formal act by which the woman became legally the man's wife; unfaithfulness on her part was adultery and punishable as such; if the relation was dissolved, a bill of divorce was required. Some time elapsed after the bridegroom claimed the fulfillment of the agreement before the bride was taken to her husband's house and the marriage consummated. The term employed for betrothal, *kiddushin*, has religious associations; it is an act by which the woman is, so to speak, consecrated to her husband, set apart for him exclusively.[20]

Betrothal was, therefore, an actual contract of marriage awaiting its final completion (which typically would take place sometime within a year of the betrothal) during which the husband would bring his wife into his home.

As the ancient historian Philo summarizes in a pithy one liner: "Betrothal has the force of matrimony."[21]

With this in mind, we can now better understand the unique circumstances regarding the betrothal and marriage between Joseph and Mary, as well the intense difficulties experienced by the Just Man by what happens *between* the time of marriage part one and part two with the Virgin of Nazareth.

We read at the beginning of Matthew's Gospel:

> When his mother Mary was betrothed to Joseph, but before they lived together, she was found with child through the Holy Spirit. Joseph, her husband, since he was a just man, yet unwilling to expose her to shame, decided to divorce her quietly. Such was his intention when behold, an angel of the Lord appeared to him in a dream and said, "Joseph, son of David, do not be afraid to take Mary your wife into your home. For it is through the Holy Spirit that this child has been conceived in her (Mt 1:18-21).

We see revealed here that Joseph and Mary began their legal marriage with their betrothal, as was typical Jewish custom. It was therefore between the time of their betrothal (marriage, part one) and the subsequent entrance of Mary into the home of Joseph (marriage, part two), that the Archangel Gabriel would appear to Mary with the most important question any human being has been asked in all human history: *Would you be God's mother?*

So Mary was legally married to Joseph when the Annunciation occurred, although not yet living in the house of her husband. This is, incidentally, why it would be technically incorrect to say that Mary became an "unwed mother" as a result of her yes to the angel Gabriel. It is more correct to say that Mary became a *married virginal mother* in virtue of her *fiat* to God's historic invitation.

Now, a key question often pops up: "If Joseph and Mary never had marital relations (which they didn't — that discussion yet to come), then how could they be truly married?"

To answer this question, we need to get to the heart of what marriage really is. The essence of marriage is, first of all, the *consent* of the couple before God to live in holy matrimony for the rest of their lives, according to the proper goals of marriage. It is not first the consummation of the marriage through sexual relations. Remember, you first need something present (in this case, the marital bond) in order to "consummate" or "confirm" that something.

Saint Ambrose, the great 4th-century Father of the Church, explains the primacy of marital consent over marital relations this way:

> The woman espoused to the man receives the name of wife, for when marriage is entered upon, then the title of marriage is acquired. The loss of virginity does not bring about marriage, but the marriage contract does. When a maiden is united, then marriage exists, not when she is known by union with her husband.[22]

The great St. Augustine confirms both the true marriage between Joseph and Mary, as well as the nature of marriage itself, in this famous passage:

Every good of marriage was fulfilled in the parents
of Christ: offspring, loyalty, and the sacraments. We
recognize the offspring in our Lord Jesus Christ
himself; the loyalty in that no adultery occurred;
and the indissolubility because no divorce. Only
conjugal intercourse did not take place.

So, not only are Joseph and Mary truly married,
but their marriage becomes the ultimate example for all
Christian marriages, which require the self-control of
chastity (though not virginity) as a foremost virtue to ensure
the full respect of both spouses in their mutual submission
and service to Christ.

The 'Doubt'

Now, let's get to the issue of what's been historically referred
to as the "doubt" of St. Joseph. The so-called "doubt"
refers to St. Joseph's response to the undeniable fact that his
betrothed began showing physical signs of being with child.

Before the angel appears in a dream to clarify
things, we can only imagine the confusion, anguish, and
unresolved questions circling in the mind and heart of the
humble carpenter. Where did the unborn child come from?
Certainly not from him. Mary is so pure and good. How
could it be possible that she would be unfaithful? That,
too, seems impossible to him since he knows and loves the
most pure Virgin. What an untold crisis fueled by such
unresolved questions must have troubled the heart of the
Just One regarding the heart of the Immaculate One!

Great Christian writers across the centuries have
posited three classic possibilities regarding Joseph's inner
response to the reality of the unborn baby in the womb of
his betrothed.

First possibility: Joseph thought that Mary had actually committed adultery and therefore sought to divorce her quietly. (Even in this potential response, we see the extraordinary virtue of the "Just Man.") Jewish law required that Joseph dismiss Mary. He could either have her appear publicly in court or he could use a private forum. If he opted to use the public forum to divorce her, Jewish law permitted the stoning to death of the woman for adultery, with the added result that full culpability for the adultery and the resulting unborn child would be placed on the woman and not on the husband. To exercise the second option, that is, to divorce her quietly, meant both that Mary would no longer be subject to being stoned to death, but also that Joseph could potentially share in the blame for a child being conceived *before* the second part of marriage had taken place. His choice to dismiss Mary quietly, even before any clarification comes from the angel, shows how righteous, humble, and sacrificial Joseph's decision was.

Second possibility: Joseph realized that this was the Messiah in the womb of Mary, and therefore, out of humility, he sought to excuse and distance himself from such a holy event as the coming of the Chosen One. He did not perceive himself to be worthy of being so closely connected to the coming of the Messiah.

Third possibility: Joseph was confused or "stupefied" by a situation that seemed as though it simply could not be reasonably explained. He was not the father. The pure Virgin could not have been unfaithful. Yet, the unborn baby's presence was undeniable. There seemed to be no viable human explanation, so he would part from her, which was required by a righteous following of the Jewish law, in a quiet manner that would not bring any scandal or hardship to his betrothed.

The vast majority of Church writers have accepted and taught that the third possibility was St. Joseph's authentic response to the virginal conception of the unborn Jesus. It has classically been referred to as the theory of "Joseph's Stupefaction." As the 16th century Josephite theologian Francisco Suarez explains:

> Joseph was unable to judge or suspect the Virgin harshly. Influenced in one direction by the factual evidence he perceived, but swayed in the other by the exalted sanctity of the Virgin as he knew it from experience, he withheld all judgment because he was overwhelmed by a kind of stupefaction and great wonder ... . Consequently, he was unwilling to expose Mary; but since for him nothing in the matter was sufficiently clear, he believed that it pertained to justice to be separated from such a woman and to dismiss her quietly.[24]

Not only was Joseph "just" to his betrothed wife under such conditions, he was truly heroic.

I believe that the third explanation of St. Joseph's stupefaction to be the most generally accurate. It is also, incidentally, the theory most consistently confirmed in the mystical tradition of the Church as manifested in saints and mystics' private revelations and writings concerning the Just Man.

Saint Joseph was not "just" a "just man." He was a righteous man, a holy man, and a saintly spouse *whose justice was perfected in mercy, patience, and humility.*

In fact, in his commentary on the infancy narratives, Pope Benedict XVI confirms that to call Joseph a "just man" means far more than only the classic moral virtue of fairly giving to his neighbor what he or she deserves. The term "just man" constitutes an expression that summarizes *an entire life of extraordinary righteousness or holiness*, lived faithfully in accordance to Old Testament Law and Scripture. The term, moreover, connects St. Joseph to the great "just men" of the Old Testament. As Pope Benedict explains:

> The designation of Joseph as a just man (*zaddik*) extends far beyond the decision he makes at this moment: it gives an overall picture of St. Joseph and at the same time it aligns him with the great figures of the Old Covenant — beginning with Abraham, the Just. If we may say that the form of piety found in the New Testament can be summed up in the expression "a believer," then the Old Testament idea of a whole life lived according to sacred Scripture is summed up in the idea of "a just man."[25]

Through the powerful intercession of this most righteous of men, may we strive to be as "just" as this Just Man was to our spouses, our family members, and all those whom we encounter, especially in times of difficulty, withholding judgment and erring in the direction of Christian mercy and love.

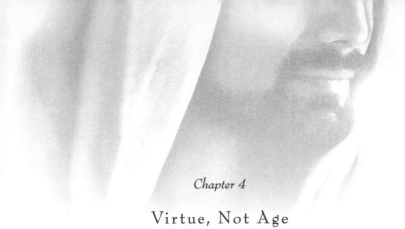

Chapter 4

Virtue, Not Age

St. Joseph's Age

"How old was St. Joseph when he married Mary?" At first glance, this question seems a bit arbitrary. What difference does it make how old Joseph was at the time of his marriage, or for that matter, any time thereafter? We don't typically ask how old most of the New Testament figures were at key moments of their lives. For example, we don't ask about the age of Saul when he became Paul, or about the age of Peter when he became the first pope. Why is St. Joseph's age at the time of his marriage to the Virgin of Nazareth an issue?

It's an issue because Joseph's age has been associated in a rather questionable way with a key dogma of the Catholic Church: the perfect, perpetual virginity of Mary.

As early Christian writers sought to defend the revealed doctrine that Mary was virginal before, during, and after the birth of Jesus (a Christian dogma proclaimed by St. Pope Martin I in 649[26]), the issue of St. Joseph's age was brought to the forefront.

Centuries before the papal proclamation of Mary's threefold virginity, a number of "apocryphal" (non-canonical) writings circulated within the early Church. These "Apocrypha" were writings about the life of Jesus, Mary, Joseph, and other related New Testamental persons and events that were not inspired biblical writings. More often than not, these apocryphal writings included significant inaccuracies, legends, and sometimes entirely fabricated episodes surrounding the true Gospel events recorded by Matthew, Mark, Luke, and John. A number of the apocryphal writings contain alleged events from the life of St. Joseph, including some real whoppers of falsified tales regarding the humble carpenter.

Some of the authors of the early Apocrypha, with good (though misguided) intentions, sought to defend authentic Christian truths, such as Mary's perpetual virginity, by recording false ideas circulating at the time concerning the life of St. Joseph. Two such apocryphal misconceptions include: (1) St. Joseph was as an extremely elderly man at the time of his marriage with Mary; and (2) St. Joseph had been married previously before his marriage to the Virgin Mary and was thereby a widower with several children from that first marriage

First, we examine the idea that St. Joseph was extremely old at the time of his marriage with the young Virgin. Why did the apocryphal writings promote this idea? Again, the intention was to safeguard the doctrine of Mary's perpetual virginity. The writers reasoned that an extremely old St. Joseph would not consider having marital relations with his approximately 16-year-old wife, so his advanced age would safeguard Mary's virginity.

Let's look at examples from some of the actual apocryphal texts. The *Protovevangelium of James* (2nd century) puts on the lips of Joseph the following words, "I am an old man, and she is a young girl."[27] The *Gospel of Pseudo-Matthew* (4th century) ascribes similar words to St. Joseph, who is quoted as saying, "I am an old man and have children; why do you hand me over to this infant, who is younger than my grandsons?"[28] The Coptic *History of St. Joseph the Carpenter* (4th-5th centuries) has St. Joseph's age recorded at 91 at the time of his marriage to the young Virgin, and his death at the vintage age of 111! Later medieval poems and plays, which were based on these early apocryphal sources, had St. Joseph's age set at 80, 120, and in several other instances, an unbelievable 200 years old!

Not only is there absolutely no foundation for Joseph's advanced age from Scripture or Tradition, but it would seem to defeat one major reason why God wanted Mary to have a husband: namely, to give the appearance of ordinary family life and for the public honor of both mother and son. But to designate an "ancient" husband to betroth and wed a 15- or 16-year-old wife would have drawn unusual, undue, and unpleasant attention to the Holy Family during its divinely designed "hidden years." The Messiah would reveal himself at the appointed time, not through an extremely unusual parental age discrepancy.

The same holds true for the second dubious idea that surfaces from the Apocrypha: that Joseph was a widower with several children at the time of his marriage to the Virgin Mary. Without any basis in the *authentic* Gospel accounts (or any other inspired source — Old Testament, New Testament, or Apostolic Tradition), this erroneous theory comes forth from various apocryphal writings.

For example, the *Gospel of Pseudo-Matthew* claims that Joseph was not only a widower but that he had already had grandchildren before his betrothal to Mary.[29] The *History of Joseph the Carpenter* suggests that Judas, James, Justus, and Simon are the literal biological sons of Joseph.[30]

Why the invention of a first marriage for Joseph? Here, we have yet another misplaced effort to defend Mary's perpetual virginity, an effort that likely arose from the fact that heretical sects at the time of the early Church were denying the virginity of Mary. The hypothesis of a first marriage of St. Joseph and subsequent children would allegedly explain the biblical references to the "brethren of the Lord" mentioned in the Gospels[31] and would thereby attempt to protect the doctrine of Mary's perpetual virginity from the allegation that Mary had other children by Joseph after the birth of Jesus.

There are two massive problems with the apocryphal theory of Joseph having had a first marriage: 1) it has no foundation in Scripture or Apostolic Tradition; 2) it seeks *to protect the virginity of Mary at the cost of the virginity of Joseph.*

From early on in the life of the Church, the apocryphal writings were seen as less than reputable and not worthy of respect. For example, Origen, the 3rd-century Christian author, acknowledged that the entire reason for the theory of Joseph's first marriage was merely an apologetic effort to protect Mary's virginity:

> Induced by the report of the Gospel named after Peter or the *Book of James,* some affirm that the brethren of Jesus are the sons of Joseph from a former wife whom he wedded before Mary. However, those who make this assertion ultimately wish to safeguard the dignity of Mary's virginity in order that the body chosen to minister to the Word … might never know man's consortship.[32]

Origen went on to speak harshly about these apocryphal works and to reassure the faithful that the only authentic Gospels are those four that have been approved by the Church.[33]

Saint Jerome, the renowned early Church Father and Scripture scholar, put forth a spirited defense of both Mary's virginity and the virginity of St. Joseph in the face of erroneous apocryphal opinions to the contrary:

> Certain people have perversely conjectured that Mary had other sons, for they assert that he alone who is to be called "first-born" has brothers. However, it is customary in holy Scripture to call "firstborn" not him whom brothers follow, but him who is first begotten … . But just as we do not deny what is written, we do reject what is not written. That God was born of a virgin we believe because we read it. That Mary consummated marriage after her childbirth we do not believe because we do not read it. … You say that Mary did not remain a virgin; even more do I claim that Joseph also was virginal through Mary, in order that from a virginal marriage a virginal son might be born … . He who merited to be called the father of the Lord remained virginal with [Mary].[34]

The Venerable Bede (7th century) would confirm the mutual virginity of Joseph and Mary, which was the conviction of St. Jerome and many other Church preachers and writers of the first Christian millennium:

> May God grant us to perceive with pious Catholic attitude that the parents of our Redeemer were

continually distinguished by unimpaired virginity, and that according to Scriptural custom, the brethren of the Lord were named as cousins and not as sons.[35]

Even though some Greek Fathers, as well as a few Latin authors, were influenced by teachings about St. Joseph in the original apocryphal writings, by the 11th century, the virginity of St. Joseph was not only the clear consensus of theological opinion but also a "belief in the Church" as attested to by the 11th century Doctor of the Church St. Peter Damien: "Not only the mother is a virgin, there remains the belief of the Church that he who served as the father is also a virgin."[36]

Before we conclude this chapter about St. Joseph's age and virtue, let's look at one seemingly unrelated issue: *How exactly was Joseph selected to be the husband of Mary?*

A Symbol of St. Joseph's Purity

It is an ancient Christian tradition, confirmed in Christian liturgy, that Mary was educated in the temple from the time she was a 3-year-old girl. At the end of her education, while still a virgin and now a young woman, Mary was to be joined in betrothal/marriage to a man from the lineage of David, a lineage shared with this unique virgin who was particularly known and revered for her extraordinary sanctity.

At a public gathering of men from the line of David, according to the ancient tradition, each suitor brought a "shoot" or branch by which the prospective husband for the Virgin Mary would be selected through some manner of the casting of lots. At a key moment in the process, the rod of Joseph was said to have miraculously blossomed.

Thus, the high priests of the temple recognized the will of God: Joseph was to wed this exceptional temple virgin. Whether or not every detail of this account is entirely accurate, it is the common consensus of many a Christian writer that a miracle was probably used to unite Mary and Joseph in holy matrimony for an event as historically sublime as the Incarnation.[37]

The tradition of the blossoming shoot has been handed on from the early Church and into the Middle Ages through its depiction in sacred art. In fact, almost every statue and painting of St. Joseph during that period commemorates the "miraculous selection" by having a blossoming shoot in the hand of St. Joseph. Eventually, the blooming branch was replaced by the lily — the universal Christian symbol of purity.

All the above Christian revelation, theology, and history lead us to the following conclusion: *Virtue, not age, safeguarded the virginity of the Immaculate Mother of God.* And so, Joseph's virginity need not be sacrificed for Mary's virginity. Grace, virtue, and love were sufficient for him and for her.

Grace, virtue, and love must also be sufficient for us as we strive — however imperfectly but perseveringly — to live lives of chastity and self-control, each according to our own God-given vocation in life.

Chapter 5

Joseph's Role in the Biblical Events

What's the highest pressure job you can think of? General of an army? President of a country? CEO of a massive international company?

What about being responsible for protecting and safeguarding the Redeemer of the entire human race, especially at his most vulnerable time — as a child?

Let's complicate the scenario even more. Let's say the "local government" put out an official order to their military (or perhaps their version of the "FBI" or Secret Service) to have this child killed. You, however, have an order from God himself to protect this child from this horrific evil, and all other potential attacks, until he enters adulthood.

Not only does every living human being depend on you doing your job for his or her eternal salvation, but, in fact, *every human being who has ever lived, is living, or will live in the future depends on you doing your job well.*

Now, that's a little pressure.

This is what it concretely means to have the God-given vocation to be the *Guardian of the Redeemer.*

Since God always gives us the graces and talents necessary to fulfill whatever vocation he's given to us, this gives us a little hint of the unparalleled graces and talents (after those given to his wife) that were granted to the Just Man to fulfill his pre-eminent task as the protector of Jesus and "head" of the Holy Family.

Scripture speaks of several events that reveal the role of St. Joseph as guardian of Jesus and head of the holiest family that ever lived. These events include: those surrounding the nativity, including the adoration of the shepherds in St. Joseph's presence (Lk 2:16); St. Joseph's naming of Jesus (Mt 1:25; Lk 2:21); St. Joseph's role in the presentation of the Infant Jesus in the Temple (Lk 2:22-36); the angel's instruction to St. Joseph to flee to Egypt and later to return to Israel (Mt 2:19-23); and St. Joseph's role in the losing and finding of the Child Jesus in the Temple (Mt 2:41-52). Let's briefly take a look at these sublime biblical events and the Just Man's role in them.

The Nativity

From the first coming of the Word and the revelation of the Redeemer to the world, *St. Joseph is present.*

After the angel appears to the shepherds, they go to Bethlehem to see the marvel of the Messiah revealed by the celestial being: "So they went in haste to find Mary and Joseph with the infant lying in the manger" (Lk 2:16).

Yes, presence is important. A father of a young family recently asked me what I thought were the most important things a father should do for his family. After Catholic formation, my answer was "presence." A father has to be present to his family, especially to his children during their teenage years, so that when they have a question or are observing a behavior (most of formation is by imitation), the father is *there* for his children.

From the beginning of the Incarnation of the God-man, St. Joseph was present, and this strong but gentle, protective presence was perpetually felt by his wife and his Child, granting to them security and peace.

Joseph manifests his true fatherly (though virginal) relation to the Savior by naming the Child "Jesus," as was the custom for the father to do, according to Jewish law: "He [Joseph] had no relations with her [Mary] until she bore a son, and he [Joseph] named him Jesus" (Mt 1:25). As the legitimate head of the family, only a true father names his child.

The Presentation in the Temple

Saint Joseph continues his paternal presence with the Infant Child and his mother during the ritual presentation of the Infant Jesus in the Temple (see Lk 2:22-36). Joseph is part of the ceremony of the presentation of his Child. He also hears firsthand the prophecy given by the elderly Simeon about this Child, who will be a "sign of contradiction" for the world, as well as the words directed toward his wife — the woman who would become the human co-redemptrix with the divine Redeemer at Calvary: "And a sword will pierce through your own heart, too" (Lk 2:35).

Here, we can only imagine the suffering that would enter the pure heart of the Just Man. He has just heard from Simeon a confirmation concerning Jesus and Mary of what he certainly already knew and had discussed with Mary in light of the Old Testament prophecies about the Savior-Messiah to come: that he would be the "Suffering Servant," whom the prophet Isaiah describes as being so disfigured in fulfilling his work of redemption that he would be hardly recognizable.[38] Thus, Joseph would carry in his heart for the rest of his life the pain of knowing that these two members of his family would undergo the greatest suffering of human history, and yet he could do nothing to prevent it. This is where the protective paternal instincts of the Guardian of the Redeemer had to give way to the perfect providence of the Heavenly Father.

From the revelation in the Temple onwards, Joseph would carry in his heart the awareness of the future suffering of the Redeemer and the Co-redemptrix. He would pray and offer his sufferings for the strength, courage, and perseverance of the New Adam and the New Eve in their redemptive mission to restore the life of grace for the human family. Was he aware that when the time of Calvary would come, he himself would not be alive to see it and that he would be unable to protect or console the Son and the Mother? Surely, at some point in the hidden life and discussions of the Holy Family at Nazareth, St. Joseph was made aware of the fact that he would not be present for his Child and his wife during their most horrendous hour. The mystical tradition of the Church suggests that this suffering of the heart of St. Joseph would contribute more than any other human suffering, after that of Jesus and Mary, to the redemption of the world.[39]

The Flight into Egypt

We then see in Scripture that Joseph is warned in a dream to take "the child and his mother" and flee to a foreign land, Egypt, as Herod's soldiers seek the death of the divine Infant:

> When they [the Magi] had departed, behold the angel of the Lord appeared to Joseph in a dream and said, "Rise, take the child and his mother and flee to Egypt, and stay there until I tell you. Herod is going to search for the child to destroy him."

Joseph rose and took the child and his mother by night and departed for Egypt (Mt 2:13-15).

Notice that, in a household made up of three of the most extraordinary people in human history (first, God the Son made man, the divine Messiah of the human race; second, the greatest creature in all history, the immaculately conceived, Co-redemptrix of the human race, Mediatrix of all graces, and world's greatest human advocate; third, a man with a fallen yet redeemed nature), God designated "person-number-three," St. Joseph, as the human authority in service of this special family. More specifically, notice that, among these three, it was to St. Joseph alone that God the Father sent his angel to warn of the impending danger of death from Herod.

What does this tell us? It tells us that God the Father respected the role of St. Joseph as the head of the Holy Family, even in a family that contained far superior beings than Joseph. Clearly, through his divine action, the Heavenly Father establishes St. Joseph's role as the providential leader of the holiest family that ever lived. This also tells us that the role of a father and husband *as the head of the family* is not based on a greater degree of holiness but simply on the will of God in assigning to this role the primary authority within the family.

Clearly in this case, St. Joseph is not the holiest member of his family. In fact, he would take the third and last place if holiness were a competition. Still, God the Father has given the husband and father of the family the role of the family's head, and he will not deprive St. Joseph of it. The Angel of the Lord is sent to this family's authority, and the grace is given to Joseph to make the correct prudential decisions in order to practically implement the directives of the angel.

This is also true for families today. In spite of contemporary experimentations, the nature of the family unit has not changed in the providential eyes and perfect will of the Heavenly Father. The nature of the human person has not changed, nor has the true nature of the family unit. The Christian husband and father remains the "head" of the family, and the Christian wife and mother is the "heart" of the family. It is God's will that husbands and fathers take humbly but seriously their God-given responsibility to be the authorities who properly serve their families, even if they are not the "first" in Christian holiness (though Christian holiness should always be their goal).

The simple principle remains: God always provides the necessary graces for the proper fulfillment of the vocations he assigns to us, and that includes the role of the husband and father as the contemporary family's leader in love and service.

The Return from Egypt

After the time of Herod, the Angel of the Lord returned to the head of the Holy Family in another dream with the instruction to return to the Promised Land:

> When Herod had died, behold the angel of the Lord appeared in a dream to Joseph in Egypt and said, "Rise, take the child and his mother and go to the land of Israel, for those who sought the child's life are dead." He rose, took the child and his mother, and went to the land of Israel. But when he heard that Archelaus was ruling over Judea in the place of his father, Herod, he was afraid to go back there.

And because he had been warned in a dream, he departed for the region of Galiliee (Mt 2:19-22).

We see here the angel's instructions and Joseph's wisdom combining for the optimal safety of the Savior and his mother. It was the prudence of Joseph upon hearing of the presence of Archelaus, the most brutal of Herod's sons, as ruler in the place of his father that led the Redeemer's Guardian to decide not to return to Bethlehem. He is subsequently instructed through yet another dream to go to Galilee.

In his commentary on the infancy narratives, Pope Benedict XVI reminds us that Joseph's receptivity to these instructive heavenly dreams reveals the Just Man's capacity to "perceive the divine":

> Once again, this shows us an essential quality of the figure of St. Joseph: his capacity to perceive the divine and his ability to discern. Only a man who is inwardly watchful for the divine, only someone with a real sensitivity for God and his ways, can receive God's message in this way.[40]

Appreciate here the remarkable trust that the Heavenly Father had in St. Joseph — a trust that would allow this human being to make his own decisions in seeking the best way to protect the young, divine Redeemer of the world. What a testimony to the sublime grace and wisdom with which the Heavenly Father endowed the earthly father of Jesus who would merit such trust.

Finding in the Temple

During the losing and subsequent "finding" of the Child Jesus in the Temple, we see the critical presence of Christ's moral father. After realizing that Jesus had not returned with either mother or father, Joseph and Mary return to the temple to find the 12-year-old Jesus sitting among the teachers of the Temple and asking them questions. Mary's words are replete with meaning when she says, "Son, why have you treated us so? Behold, *your father*[41] and I have been looking for you anxiously" (Lk 2:48).

Mary refers to Joseph in speaking with the young Jesus with the title "your father." The Sacred Word of God, delivered from the lips of the Immaculate Mother, properly refers to St. Joseph as the "father" of Jesus because, as we shall see, the deepest meaning of fatherhood is not biological but *moral and relational.*

Saint Pope John Paul II in his Apostolic Letter *Redemptoris Custos (Guardian of the Redeemer)* explains that in Jesus' response to his parents in the Temple, St. Joseph was again reminded that he was, by divine decree, the "guardian of the mystery of God":

> Joseph, of whom Mary had just used the words "your father," heard this answer. That, after all, is what all the people said and thought: Jesus was "the son" (as was supposed) of "Joseph" (Lk 3:23). Nonetheless the reply of Jesus in the Temple brought once again to the mind of his "presumed father" what he had heard on that night twelve years earlier: "Joseph ... do not fear to take Mary as your wife, *for that which is conceived of her is of the Holy Spirit.*" From that time onward he knew that

he was a guardian of the mystery of God, and it was *precisely this mystery* that the twelve-year-old *Jesus brought to mind*: "I must be in my Father's house.

"A guardian of the mystery of God." Amazing. Only a few men in human history could make that kind of claim. And only one man could make the claim to be the very "Guardian of the Redeemer" himself.

Chapter 6

Virginal Father of the Savior

What's the essence of true fatherhood? Is it physical or biological? Or does it have even more to do with the relationship of the child to a man he or she calls "father"?

When, for example, a baby is adopted from an orphanage and enters a family with a husband and wife, and the husband takes that child, treats him or her as his own, loves, supports, and protects the child, we clearly call that man the "father" of the child — and rightly so.

Now it may be objected, "But that man was not the biological father of the child." Yes, that is true. Yet that man is rightly called the "father" of that adopted child because he beautifully and generously fulfilled every aspect of authentic fatherhood, except for the biological dimension. He is not father of the child physically, but by virtue of his *relationship* to his adopted child, he possesses a true and legally recognized fatherhood.

I think we would all agree that the *fullness* of human fatherhood extends beyond the physical to the relational: What man raised me? What man protected and supported me? What man was there for me? What man loved me? The adopted child, from his perspective of having received for many years the love and paternal protection of this man, is the first to proudly, publicly, and gratefully proclaim, "Of course, that man is my father!"

That's why a pretty good case can be made that beyond just the biological dimension, the essence of authentic fatherhood lies in the fulfillment of a relationship of love, support, and protection between the man and the child.

St. Joseph's Fatherhood

From this perspective, we can now examine the fundamental question: *Can St. Joseph be called the true father of Jesus?*

First, we must see the critical importance of stating without confusion that St. Joseph is in no way the biological father of Jesus.

To erroneously see St. Joseph as the biological father of Jesus is to threaten the very divinity of Jesus. The Holy Spirit, not Joseph, is the divine source of the conception of Jesus Christ. As the 4th century Nicene Creed states, Jesus was "conceived by the Holy Spirit, born of the Virgin Mary." The *Word*, the Second Person of the Trinity, became flesh, not through the cooperation of man but through the immediate action of God.

This is what some ancient Christian writers were seeking to defend when they were hesitant to ascribe to St. Joseph a true "fatherhood" of Jesus. For example, the early Christian author St. Epiphanius writes in response to the heretical teaching of Joseph being Jesus' biological father:

> Although Jesus was supposed to be the son of Joseph, He is by no means the son in reality; rather, this Joseph occupied the place of a father because so it pleased God, but he was not the father … . Even though according to the flesh Joseph had

absolutely nothing to do with the origin of the Savior, he was held as his father because of a definite providential reason.[42]

As these early heresies about Joseph's physical fatherhood were responded to and eventually died down, the Church Fathers began to appreciate the relational fatherhood of the Just Man to Jesus — a true, though, once again, virginal fatherhood based on the love, protection, support, sacrifice, and service that St. Joseph offered to Jesus. The master articulator of this truth within the first centuries of the Church was the great St. Augustine.

Saint Augustine established the legitimacy of calling Joseph the "Virginal father" of Jesus through both his relationship to Mary as husband and his relationship to Jesus. Read his eloquent explanation:

A Son was born of the Virgin Mary to the piety and love of Joseph, and that son was the Son of God. Thus, should not the husband accept virginally what the wife brought forth virginally? For just as she was a virginal wife, so was he a virginal husband; just as she was a virginal mother, so was he a virginal father. Therefore, whoever says, "He should not have been called father because he did not generate the son" looks to concupiscence in the procreation of children, not to the inner sentiments of love ... .

Let his greater purity confirm his fatherhood; let not holy Mary reprehend us, for she was unwilling to place her name before that of her

husband, but said, "Thy father and I have been
seeking thee sorrowing." Therefore let no perverse
murmurers do what the virginal wife did not do ...
as he was a virginal husband, so he was a virginal
father. Just as was the man, just so was the woman.
The Holy Spirit, resting in the justice of both, gave
a son to both.[43]

Saint Augustine defends here the legitimacy of calling
the Just Man the true father of Jesus on these two solid
biblical and legal foundations: 1) Joseph gave to Jesus, in
the order of love, all that a father rightly gives his child in
a father-child relationship; 2) his wife, Mary, is the true
mother of this child, and, therefore, in light of the fact
that Joseph is married to the physical mother of Jesus, he is
legally and morally the true father of Jesus. Saint Augustine
sums it up in this succinct statement: "Because of this holy
and virginal marriage with Christ's mother, Joseph merited
to be called the very father of Christ."[44]

In sum, not only is it right for Jesus to call St. Joseph
"father" in the same sense that an adopted son calls the
man who adopts, raises, and loves him "father," but even
more is it right for Jesus to call the Just Man "father," since
he is also the man married to Jesus' physical mother.

The great St. John Chrysostom places these words
on the lips of the angel who addresses St. Joseph, which
manifest the early Church belief in Joseph's moral
fatherhood:

Mary will bring forth a son, and call his name, Jesus.
For you must think that because he is of the Holy
Spirit you are therefore excluded from cooperating

in this plan. Even though you contributed nothing to his generation and the Virgin remained inviolate, nevertheless what belongs to a father without destroying the dignity of virginity, that I bestow on you, that you name the Child. Even though he is not your physical offspring, nonetheless you will act as a father towards him.[45]

Saint Thomas Aquinas would later speak of the miraculous "moral bond" between the hearts of Jesus and St. Joseph, even without their having a biological relationship.[46] The Church's foremost theologian would go on to defend, quoting St. Augustine, why it is legitimate to call St. Joseph a true father of Jesus:

According to Augustine, Joseph is called father of Christ, just as he is called the husband of Mary, without fleshly mingling and by the sole bond of marriage; thereby being united to him much more closely than if he were adopted from another family. Consequently that Christ was not begotten of Joseph by a fleshly union is no reason why Joseph should not be called father, since he would be the father even of an adopted child not born of his wife.[47]

The 17th century French spiritual writer, Bossuet, would speak of the Heavenly Father's infusion of a "spark" of his own divine love of Jesus into Joseph's heart, which gave rise to Joseph's confidence in having authority, as a human, over his divine Son:

The same divine hand which fashions each man's heart gave a father's heart to Joseph and a son's heart to Jesus, so that Jesus obeyed Joseph and Joseph did not fear to command Jesus. It was because Christ's true Father had chosen Joseph to act as father to his Son in this world. And in so doing God had, as it were, charged Joseph's breast with some ray or spark of his own boundless love for his Son. It was this that aroused a father's love in Joseph; so much so that, feeling a father's heart burn within him, Joseph also felt that God was telling him to use a father's authority.[48]

The 19th century papal Magisterium added key authoritative confirmation of the fatherhood of St. Joseph. Pope Leo XIII offered an elegant summation on the legitimacy of referring to the Just Man as "father of the Word Incarnate":

No one is unaware that Blessed Joseph was chosen by the special providence of God in preference to all other creatures in order that he might merit to be the husband of the Virgin Mother of God and to be the father of the Word Incarnate, not indeed by generation, but by love, by adoption, and by the right of marriage. So much so is this a fact that we read that he was not only called the father of Christ in the holy gospels and by the Blessed Virgin herself, but also that the Lord Jesus Christ in the days of his flesh humbly deigned to be subject to him as a father. ...[49]

As remarkable as it is for a fallen yet redeemed human being to be rightly called the virginal "father" of the Second Person of the Trinity made man, we can also say something about Joseph's relationship to the Heavenly Father within his vocation of fatherhood.

In a real sense, St. Joseph was a kind of living icon of God the Father to Jesus while he was on earth.

Of course, St. Joseph was human, and because of original sin, he was conceived outside of the family of God. Still, God the Father, to prepare Joseph for his vocation as Christ's moral father, infused into this man the greatest of his own paternal virtues so Jesus would experience the best human father the world had to offer.

Simply put: *Saint Joseph was the world's greatest father, who, to the highest degree, reflected the paternity of God the Father himself.*

This is why in our present age of "father deprivation," we do well to return to the witness of St. Joseph for today's husbands and fathers.

To imitate the fatherhood of St. Joseph is ultimately to imitate the Fatherhood of God himself.

I'm sure Jesus, before all others in heaven, would be the first to proudly, publicly, and gratefully say of the man who was married to his mother, the man who raised him, loved him, protected him, and sacrificed for him for his entire life: "Of course, that man is my father."

Chapter 7

To Love the Just Man

Within God the Father's mysterious providence, he sometimes waits far longer than we would prefer to bless the Church and the world with his *special gifts*. Typically, the "best wine" is the one that has aged the longest.

We, in our impatience, want the "best wine" immediately. God knows the best timing for all of his gifts in order for them to reach and be received into the hearts of humanity.

Such was the case with the Church's appreciation of the gift of St. Joseph.

There has never been a time in the Church without at least some acknowledgement and love of the Just Man. For example, St. Joseph is depicted in the catacombs in various Magi scenes and in St. Mary Major's Basilica (5th century) in numerous mosaics. The early historian Nicephorus states that St. Helena had a church erected in the Holy Land in honor of St. Joseph. In the 7th century, the town of Nazareth had two great churches: one honoring the Annunciation and a second honoring St. Joseph, Our Lady, and the Christ Child's original dwelling place.[50]

St. Joseph's inclusion in some local liturgies on March 19 in the West is documented in martyrologies (which told

the stories of saints, martyrs, and confessors) that date back
to the 9[51] century. The first liturgical feast in honor of
Joseph appears in the East around 1000 A.D.[52]

Still, it wasn't until later in the Church's history
that devotion to St. Joseph took on its present universal,
pre-eminent dimension. The Heavenly Father knew that
the Church of the Middle Ages and beyond would be in
particular need of a developed love and understanding of St.
Joseph above all other saints, except for his wife. He knew
the need for the universal intercession and protection of
the moral father of Christ for the entire Church and world,
especially in medieval and modern times.

Let's take a look at some expressions of the love for
the Just Man found in the testimonies of medieval minds
and hearts.

We begin with the great Franciscan preacher St.
Bernadine of Siena who, in the following excerpt from one
of his 15th-century sermons, manifests a more developed
level of devotion to our great saint:

> Whenever the divine favor chooses someone for a
> special grace or an exalted position, it endows the
> person thus chosen with all the gifts necessary for
> him and for his task. This was pre-eminently verified
> in St. Joseph, the foster father of Jesus Christ and
> true spouse of the Queen of Heaven and Mistress of
> Angels. He was chosen by the Father as the faithful
> foster father and guardian of his principal treasures,
> that is, His son and His spouse. If you compare
> him to the whole Church of Christ, is he not that
> chosen and unique man through whom and under
> whom Christ was brought into the world with due

order and honor? If then, the entire holy Church is in debt to the Virgin Mother, because, through her, she was made worthy to receive Christ, after Mary, she owes him gratitude and singular veneration. For he is the key of the Old Testament, in whom the dignity of the patriarchs and the prophets attain its promised fruit. ... There can be no doubt that in heaven Christ did not deny Joseph that familiarity, reverence, and exalted dignity which he tendered him as a Son to his father while he lived among men. He rather increased and perfected it.[53]

Notice the substantial development from the early Church acknowledgment of St. Joseph as part of devotion to the Holy Family to the medieval witness to him as the man most graced by God to fulfill his unparalleled vocation as the father of Jesus and intercessor for the entire Church.

This Middle Age expansion in love for St. Joseph is strongly fostered by the writings of another 15th-century author, Fr. John Gerson, chancellor of the University of Paris. This French teacher and preacher wrote the celebrated *Considerations on St. Joseph*, an extensive Latin poem that expounded upon St. Joseph's sanctity and virtues.

Gerson also delivered a notable sermon on St. Joseph during the Council of Constans in the early 15th century, in which he called the Council fathers to officially invoke St. Joseph's intercession for the Church (at a time of great trial because of the Western Schism) and to institute a feast of St. Joseph to obtain his powerful intercession for the Church's unity.

Gerson's starting point and the guiding principle for his theology of St. Joseph was this: Joseph was the true husband of the Mother of God. For Gerson, all of Joseph's other extraordinary virtues and gifts flowed from this fundamental principle.

This French preacher maintained that St. Joseph was pre-sanctified in his mother's womb (similar to St. John the Baptist); that his sanctity reached higher than the angelic choirs of Seraphim and Cherubim (by virtue of his "proximity" or closeness to Jesus and Mary); and that he was the protector of the Church (which set the foundation for the later papal declarations of St. Joseph as "Patron of the Universal Church").[54]

Here's just one example of the beauty of Gerson's teachings concerning Joseph and his relationship to Jesus:

> Joseph was the father of Jesus Christ in the people's opinion, father in his solicitude as foster parent, and father in the generation — not of course on his own part but on the part of his wife, Mary, in whom the Holy Spirit worked and in a certain sense represented Joseph not with human seed but with mystical inspiration. Joseph can therefore be called father of the Child Jesus, not the actual but rather the legal father to whom the Holy Spirit raised up a seed more eminent than fleshly seed. Jesus was indeed born out of the land and property of Joseph ... . Should there not be accorded to him in preference to all other men a legal right to the praiseworthy rearing of the Child Jesus since Jesus was born in the flesh and out of the flesh whose possession was truly delivered to Joseph by the right of marriage?[55]

In the 15th century, an extensive growth in devotion to St. Joseph was visible in the liturgy. Pope Sixtus IV introduced the feast of St. Joseph to the Church in Rome; and then in churches all across Europe, the faithful began to include the Mass and Office of St. Joseph in their breviaries and missals.

Spirituality and devotional works dedicated to the Just Man in the 16th century were also considerably on the rise. The best of both came from one of the greatest Josephite devotees of all times, St. Teresa of Avila. Known as the "Doctor of the Church on Prayer," this great Carmelite reformer named 12 out of the 17 monasteries she founded after St. Joseph!

Spreading devotion to St. Joseph throughout Spain and beyond, St. Teresa is best known for her famous testimony to the power of St. Joseph's intercession and her "challenge" to all who have not yet prayed to the greatest human intercessor after Our Lady. Although it was cited at the beginning of our concise work, it is well worth a re-appreciation here:

> I wish I could persuade everyone to be devoted to the glorious St. Joseph, for I have great experience of the blessings which he can obtain from God. I do not remember that I have ever asked anything of him which he has failed to grant. I am astonished at the great favors which God has bestowed on me through this blessed saint, and at the perils from which he has delivered me, both in body and in soul.
>
> To other saints, the Lord seems to have given grace to help us in some of our necessities. But my experience is that St Joseph helps us in them all; also that the Lord wishes to teach us that, as He was

himself subject on earth to St Joseph, so in Heaven He now does all that Joseph asks. This has also been the experience of other persons whom I have advised to commend themselves to the saint ... .

I only request, for the love of God, whoever will not believe me will test the truth of what I say, for he will see by experience how great a blessing it is to recommend oneself to this glorious patriarch and to be devoted to him.[57]

Beyond this extraordinary witness to his intercession, the Great Teresa also records occasions of St. Joseph actually appearing to her. On one occasion, he appeared to her in a vision and assured her of his intercession for the funds needed for the building of her monasteries:

Once when I was in one of my difficulties, not knowing what to do and unable to pay the workmen, my true father and lord, St. Joseph, appeared to me, and gave me to understand that money would not be wanting, and I must hire the workmen.[58]

On another occasion, St. Teresa saw Our Lady and St. Joseph in an ecstatic vision, during which Our Lady praised the Carmelite for her devotion to St. Joseph:

Our Lady seemed at once to take me by both hands. She said that I pleased her very much by being devoted to the glorious St. Joseph. ... I did not see St. Joseph so distinctly, though I saw clearly that he was there.[59]

Saint Francis de Sales, another Doctor of the Church, continued to champion Josephite devotion in his classic writings *Treatise on the Love of God* and *Spiritual Conferences*, in which he eloquently describes Joseph's union with Jesus through his marriage to Mary:

> By means of the marriage between Our Lady and the glorious St. Joseph, the Good of eternal goods, Our Lord Himself, belonged to St. Joseph as well as to Our Lady. This is not true in regards to the nature which he took in the womb of our glorious mistress, and which had been formed by the Holy Spirit by the most pure blood of Our Lady, but it is true as regards grace, which made him participate in all the possessions of his blessed spouse and which increased so marvelously his growth in perfection; and this through his continual communications with Our Lady.[60]

The last example of the stellar devotion offered to St. Joseph during the end of this historical period comes from Bossuet. Bossuet authored a panegyric on St. Joseph and the three trusts committed to his protection and care: 1) the virginity of Mary; 2) the rearing of Jesus Christ; and 3) the secret of the Incarnation.

The most renowned parts of the panegyric concern his reflection on the vocation of St. Joseph being ordained by God to protect Mary's virginity and Jesus Christ himself, and the comparison and contrast he makes with Joseph's vocation and that of the apostles. In light of its ideal depiction of 17th-century Josephite spirituality, as well as its truth and beauty, let's enjoy an extended quote from this classic work:

You behold the dignity of Mary in the fact that her blessed virginity has been chosen from eternity to give Jesus Christ to the world; and you behold the dignity of Joseph in the fact that the purity of Mary, which has been of such value to our nature, has been confided to his care. It is he that preserves for the world something so needful. O Joseph, guard the trust! Guard dearly this sacred trust of Mary's purity since it has pleased the Eternal Father to protect Mary's virginity under the veil of this marriage she can no longer preserve it without you; and thus your purity has become in a fashion necessary for the world, by the glorious charge which has been given you to protect the virginity of Mary. ...

But it is not enough for the Eternal Father to have confided to Joseph the virginity of Mary. He prepares for him something even more exalted; and after having trusted to his loyalty this holy virginity which is to give Jesus Christ to the world (as if he planned to exhaust his infinite generosity in favor of the Patriarch), he is now about to place Jesus Christ himself into Joseph's hands, and he wishes him protected by Joseph's care. If we penetrate into this secret, if we enter into the depths of this mystery, there it is that we should discover something so glorious for the just man Joseph that we will never be able to understand it sufficiently! ...

Among all vocations, I discern two in the Scriptures which seem diametrically opposed. The first is that of the Apostles; the second, that of Joseph. Jesus is revealed to the apostles, Jesus is revealed to Joseph, but under very contrary conditions. He is revealed to the apostles in order to be proclaimed throughout the entire world; he is revealed to Joseph in order to be in silence and to be hidden. The apostles are lights to make Jesus visible to the world; Joseph is a veil to cover him; and under this mysterious veil, there is hidden the virginity of Mary and the magnificence of the Savior of souls. ... The holy apostles preach the gospel so valiantly that the sound of their preaching reaches even unto heaven. Joseph on the contrary, hearing the stories of the marvels of Jesus Christ, listens, admires, and is silent.[61]

Devotion based on doctrine; love based on truth. This is the foundation for the authentic Christian piety that we see offered to the virginal father of Jesus and husband of Mary during the Middle Ages.

It is the great theological and devotional Josephite development of this era that prepares a foundation for the authoritative teachings of the 19th- and 20th-century popes, who bring to full flower and confirm these sublime patristic and medieval insights.

As Church Doctors, poets, and popes all make clear: It is a good and holy thing to love the Just Man.

Chapter 8

The Popes Go to Joseph

As a beautiful crescendo stemming from the theology, spirituality, and devotion that gradually came forth from the history of the Church, the contemporary popes have laid out for us (with the unique blessing of papal authority) much more of the *whole truth* about St. Joseph.

Both in terms of doctrinal clarity and devotional generosity, the modern Holy Fathers have made clear their desire to accentuate the importance of the moral father of Jesus, *Head* of the Mystical Body, and how he has the same dynamic role and relationship *for us* — the *members* of the Mystical Body — the Church of today.

Let's highlight major statements and acts by the contemporary popes about the Just Man, beginning from the middle of the 19th century and continuing to our present day.

Now, I'd like to provide you with the actual words of the modern successors of St. Peter (even if some are a bit longer than some of the other quotes we've looked at). I do this for the following reasons: 1) They carry the weight of papal authority; 2) they comprise extraordinary summaries of essential Josephite doctrine and devotion; and 3) they enable you to spread the whole truth of St. Joseph to others during our present mission of the New Evangelization.

During the First Vatican Council, Blessed Pius IX received a significant number of petitions from superiors of religious orders, as well as from cardinals and bishops attending the Council, requesting that the Holy Father declare St. Joseph the "Patron of the Universal Church." This request came at a time of great attack on the Church from several external forces, and historians note that when Blessed Pius IX did indeed make the declaration, placing the entire Church under St. Joseph's protection, it marked the beginning of the reversal of these attacks and caused a new rise of respect for the Church in general and for the papacy in particular.[62]

During his December 8, 1870, proclamation, Blessed Pius IX became the first Pope to explicitly rank St. Joseph as second only to Our Lady in holiness and continued to speak of the appropriateness of the Church going to Joseph in times of difficulties:

> Because of the sublime dignity which God conferred on his most faithful servant, the Church has always most highly honored and praised blessed Joseph next to his spouse, the Virgin Mother of God, and has besought his intercession in times of trouble. ...[63]
>
> And now, therefore, when in these most troubled times the Church is beset with enemies on every side and is weighed down by calamities so heavy that ungodly men assert that the gates of hell have at length prevailed against her, the venerable prelates of the Catholic world have presented to the Sovereign Pontiff their own petitions and those of the faithful committed to their care, praying that he would deign to constitute St. Joseph Patron

of the Universal Church. And their prayer and desire was renewed by them even more earnestly at the Sacred Ecumenical Council of the Vatican ... accordingly it has now pleased our most holy sovereign, Pius IX, to comply with the desires of the prelates and to commit to St. Joseph's most powerful patronage himself and all the faithful. He therefore has declared St. Joseph Patron of the Universal Church ... .[64]

Why was it so huge, so historic, that St. Joseph should be named the Universal Patron of the Church? For at least two reasons.

First, it is a unique honor that goes side by side with the Just Man being the holiest person after Mary. No one else is "patron" and "spiritual father" over the entire Church.

Second, it fully enacts the principle that what Joseph was to Jesus, Joseph is to us. As he protected Jesus during his most vulnerable time of earthly existence, St. Joseph protects us, disciples of his Son, Jesus, and members of the Church, during our most vulnerable times on earth.

In short, *St. Joseph is officially acknowledged and declared to be the entire Church's true and powerful spiritual father.*

Pope Leo XIII (Blessed Pius IX's successor), continued the historic papal honors for the Just Man by writing *Quamquam Pluries* (August 15, 1889), the first complete encyclical on the life, virtues, and sanctity of St. Joseph.

In the following extraordinary quote from this document, Leo XIII provides one of the greatest summaries of why St. Joseph deserves the title of the

Church's universal spiritual father and further explains why St. Joseph's holiness is second only to the Mother of God among of human persons.

To fully appreciate this text, let's look at a particularly celebrated passage in its entirety:

> The special motives for which St. Joseph has been proclaimed Patron of the Church, and from which the Church looks for singular benefit from his patronage and protection, are that Joseph was the spouse of Mary and that he was reputed the Father of Jesus Christ. From these sources have sprung his dignity, his holiness, his glory. In truth, the dignity of the Mother of God is so lofty that naught created can rank above it. But as Joseph has been united to the Blessed Virgin by the ties of marriage, it may not be doubted that he approached nearer than any to the eminent dignity by which the Mother of God surpasses so nobly all created natures.
>
> For marriage is the most intimate of all unions which from its essence imparts a community of gifts between those that by it are joined together. Thus in giving Joseph the Blessed Virgin as spouse, God appointed him to be not only her life's companion, the witness of her maidenhood, the protector of her honor, but also, by virtue of the conjugal tie, a participator in her sublime dignity. And Joseph shines among all mankind by the most august dignity, since by divine will, he was the guardian of the Son of God and reputed as His father among men. Hence it came about that the Word of God was humbly subject to Joseph, that He obeyed him,

and that He rendered to him all those offices that children are bound to render to their parents.

From this two-fold dignity flowed the obligation which nature lays upon the head of families, so that Joseph became the guardian, the administrator, and the legal defender of the divine house whose chief he was. And during the whole course of his life he fulfilled those charges and those duties. He set himself to protect with a mighty love and a daily solicitude his spouse and the Divine Infant; regularly by his work he earned what was necessary for the one and the other for nourishment and clothing; he guarded from death the Child threatened by a monarch's jealousy, and found for Him a refuge; in the miseries of the journey and in the bitternesses of exile he was ever the companion, the assistance, and the upholder of the Virgin and of Jesus.

Now the divine house which Joseph ruled with the authority of a father, contained within its limits the scarce-born Church. From the same fact that the most holy Virgin is the mother of Jesus Christ is she the mother of all Christians whom she bore on Mount Calvary amid the supreme throes of the Redemption; Jesus Christ is, in a manner, the firstborn of Christians, who by the adoption and Redemption are His brothers. And for such reasons the Blessed Patriarch looks upon the multitude of Christians who make up the Church as confided specially to his trust — this limitless family spread over the earth, over which, because he is the spouse of Mary and the Father of Jesus Christ he holds, as it were, a paternal authority. It is, then, natural and worthy that as the Blessed Joseph ministered to all the needs of the family at Nazareth and girt it about with his protection, he should now cover with the cloak of his heavenly patronage and defend the Church of Jesus Christ.

This magnificent teaching of Pope Leo XIII is one of the best single summaries of the special role of St. Joseph ever penned!

Of the many pearls from this passage, perhaps the greatest is the papal confirmation that "there can be no doubt that more than any other person, he approached that super-eminent dignity by which the Mother of God is raised above all created natures." Theologians have coined the term "protodulia" for this truth, namely that among all saints (except, once again, for Our Lady who rightly receives the devotion of what is called "hyperdulia"[65]), St. Joseph should be honored "first" among all other saints in the order of authentic Christian devotion.

Pope Benedict XV issued a 1920 document that established St. Joseph as the special "Patron of Workmen."[66] In his statement, Benedict XV urged devotion to St. Joseph as a remedy both for the tragic devastation suffered as a result of World War I and the subsequent, massive moral decline.

One of St. Joseph's most important patronages is his role as "Model of Workers," through which the humble carpenter of Nazareth underscores the essential dignity and value of human work. This theme (of St. Joseph as a witness to the God-given dignity of human labor) was to be a favorite theme of many a pope to come.

Benedict XV further recommends the faithful to go to Joseph as the "Patron of the Dying," encourages them to "learn from Joseph" by keeping focused in hope on the higher things of heaven during this passing life, and reminds them that he is a key to having a true devotion to the Holy Family:

> Let all persons, then, learn from Joseph to consider present passing affairs in the light of future good which will endure forever, and find consolation amid human vicissitudes in the hope of heavenly things, so that they may aspire to them in a way conformable to the divine will — that is, by living soberly, justly, and piously. ...
>
> With the increase of devotion to St. Joseph among the faithful, there will necessarily result an increase in their devotion towards the Holy Family of Nazareth, of which he was the august head, for these devotions spring spontaneously one from the other. By St. Joseph we are led directly to Mary, and by Mary to the fountain of all holiness, Jesus Christ, who sanctified the domestic virtues by His obedience to St. Joseph and Mary.[67]

Saint Joseph as the "Patron of the Dying" constitutes yet another principal patronage for the head of the Holy Family. Can you imagine dying in a more secure, dignified, and sanctified manner than in the company of the Redeemer and the Co-redemptrix who, for this man alone, also were addressed as "Son" and "wife"?

Pope Benedict XV further encourages the faithful to observe devotion to St. Joseph on all *Wednesdays of the year* (as was already the practice of the Apostolic See) and in the month of March, which is especially dedicated to him.[68] Devotion to St. Joseph on Wednesdays, and in particular on the first Wednesday of each month, becomes a recurring theme in papal recommendations and contemporary devotion.

During the frightful rise of Communism in Russia during the 1930s, Pope Pius XI responded by declaring St. Joseph to be the special Patron of the Church's struggle against Communism in his encyclical against atheistic Communism, which he intentionally released on the solemnity of St. Joseph, March 19, 1937:

> We place the vast campaign of the Church against world communism under the standard of St. Joseph, her mighty protector. He belongs to the working class, and he bore the burdens of poverty, for himself and the Holy Family, whose tender and vigilant head he was. To him was entrusted the Divine Child when Herod loosed his assassins against Him. In a life of faithful performance of everyday duties, he left an example for all those who must gain their bread by the work of their hands. He won for himself the title of the "Just," serving thus as a living model of that Christian justice which should reign in social life.[69]

Pius XI also referred to St. Joseph's "all-powerful intercession." The "omnipotence" of St. Joseph's intercession does not stem from Joseph's being "all-powerful" but rather from his extraordinary influence on his "all-powerful" divine Son, as well as upon his wife's role as the Mediatrix of all graces and universal Advocate:

> ... The intercession of St. Joseph is that of the husband, the putative father, the head of the family of Nazareth which was composed of himself, Mary, and Jesus. And as St. Joseph was truly the head or the master of that house, his intercession cannot be but all-powerful. For what could Jesus and Mary refuse to St. Joseph, he who was entirely devoted to them all his life, and to whom they truly owed the means of their earthly existence?[70]

Pope Pius XII continued the battle against Communism and secularism during the 1940s and 1950s with the Just Man at the helm.

On May 1, 1955, Pius XII declared in an address to the Christian Association of Italian Workers that May 1 would from that day onward be celebrated as the *"feast of St. Joseph the Worker."*

This was a true inspiration by the Holy Father, as May 1 had previously been a common celebration of labor in Europe. There had also been a recent hijacking of the secular holiday by the Communists, who had designated May 1 as "Communist's Worker Day."

Pius XII transformed the holiday into a *holy day* by establishing it as the feast of St. Joseph the Worker. This effectively "baptized" the feast for a true Christian celebration of the dignity of work as embodied in the saintly carpenter of Nazareth.[71] As Pius XII declared to his Christian labor audience:

We are happy to announce to you our determination
to institute — as in fact we do institute — the
liturgical feast of St. Joseph the Worker, assigning it
as the first day of May. Are you pleased with this our
gift, beloved workers? We are certain that you are,
because the humble workman of Nazareth not only
personifies before God and the Church the dignity
of the man who works with his hands, but is always
the provident guardian of you and your families.[72]

The newly canonized "Good Pope" St. John XXIII
was an exceptional devotee of St. Joseph. During his brief
pontificate, he was quick to utilize the "Patron of the
Universal Church."

In 1961, St. John XXIII released an Apostolic
Letter on St. Joseph, addressed to the world's bishops
and faithful. In this document, the Holy Father both
summarized the last century of papal devotion to the Just
Man and declared St. Joseph the *heavenly protector of the
Second Vatican Council*:

Oh! The invocation of St. Joseph! Oh! devotion
to St. Joseph for the protection of the Second
Ecumenical Council of the Vatican!

Venerable brethren and sons of Rome, brethren
and well-beloved children of the entire world! This
is what we wanted to lead up to and this is why we
are sending this Apostolic Letter on March 19. We
wanted the celebration of the Feast of St. Joseph,
the Patron of the Universal Church, to bring your
souls the inspiration for an extraordinary renewal
of fervor that will come from a more lively, more

ardent, and more constant prayer participation in the cares of the Church, your teacher and mother, instructor and guide for this extraordinary event — the 21st Ecumenical Council and the second of the Vatican ... . O St. Joseph! It is here, in this very place, that you will exercise your office of "Protector of the Universal Church."[73]

How extremely relevant are these inspired words of John XXIII for us today who seek to faithfully live out the direction of the Council within its *authentic* spirit. How much we would benefit from invoking St. Joseph to intercede for us so we can properly understand and incorporate the teachings of the Second Vatican Council, since St. Joseph was its special Patron and Protector.

As if this were not enough, Good Pope John went on to announce to the Council Fathers that the name of St. Joseph was to be inserted into the First Eucharistic Prayer of the Mass after the name of Mary. This papal move was a form of "protodulia in action," and now the Just Man's name *follows that of Mary and is before all other saints in the Roman Canon of the Mass.*

Still, some might be thinking to themselves, "Fine, popes of the last hundred years have highlighted St. Joseph. But what about *now*? Can you make a case for the relevance of St. Joseph in the 21st century?"

Absolutely. Let's hear from the late, great St. John Paul II.

On the hundredth anniversary of Leo XIII's famous encyclical (August 15, 1989), the *Totus Tuus* Pope wrote his own Apostolic Exhortation on St. Joseph, *Guardian of the Redeemer*. In this masterful papal document, St. John

Paul cited the former words of Pope Leo as being *absolutely relevant to the same type of dangers that our Church is presently facing*:

> One hundred years ago, Pope Leo XIII had already exhorted the Catholic world to pray for the protection of St. Joseph, Patron of the whole Church. The Encyclical Epistle *Quamquam Pluries* appealed to Joseph's "fatherly love ... for the child Jesus" and commended to him, as "the provident guardian of the divine Family," "the beloved inheritance which Jesus Christ purchased by his blood." Since that time — as I recalled at the beginning of this Exhortation — the Church has implored the protection of St. Joseph on the basis of "that sacred bond of charity which united him to the Immaculate Virgin Mother of God," and the Church has commended to Joseph all of her cares, including those dangers which threaten the human family.
>
> Even today we have many reasons to pray in a similar way: "Most beloved father, dispel the evil of falsehood and sin ... graciously assist us from heaven in our struggle with the powers of darkness ... and just as once you saved the Child Jesus from mortal danger, so now defend God's holy Church from the snares of her enemies and from all adversity." Today we still have good reason to commend everyone to St. Joseph.[74]

The popes of the 19th century, when faced with serious and multiform dangers, always went to Joseph. The popes of today, when faced with similarly grave and ubiquitous dangers are likewise going to Joseph.

Saint John Paul II also highlights the role and intercession of *St. Joseph as being at the heart of the New Evangelization*. No man was closer to the Incarnation of the Word than he was, and the Church's spiritual father directed us to the best way of spreading the saving mystery of the Word made flesh in the third millennium:

The Second Vatican Council made all of us sensitive once again to the "great things which God has done," and to that "economy of salvation" of which St. Joseph was a special minister. Commending ourselves, then, to the protection of him to whose custody God "entrusted his greatest and most precious treasures," let us at the same time learn from him how to be servants of the "economy of salvation." May St. Joseph become for all of us an exceptional teacher in the service of Christ's saving mission, a mission which is the responsibility of each and every member of the Church: husbands and wives, parents, those who live by the work of their hands or by any other kind of work, those called to the contemplative life and those called to the apostolate.

This just man, who bore within himself the entire heritage of the Old Covenant, was also brought into the "beginning" of the New and Eternal Covenant in Jesus Christ. May he show us the paths of this saving Covenant as we stand at the

threshold of the next millennium, in which there
must be a continuation and further development
of the "fullness of time" that belongs the ineffable
mystery of the Incarnation of the Word.

May St. Joseph obtain for the Church and for
the world, as well as for each of us, the blessing of
the Father, Son, and Holy Spirit.[75]

An increasing devotion to St. Joseph generously
continues in the Church under the *dynamic pontificate of
Pope Francis.*

Just over a month after his election, Pope Francis,
as one of his first papal acts, decreed that the name of
St. Joseph was to be inserted into Eucharistic Prayers II,
III, and IV, immediately following the invocation to the
Mother of God.[76]

Again, we see in one of Pope Francis's earliest decisions
as Pope*"protodulia" in action,* expressed in a concrete,
liturgical way.

The Just Man is so dear to the heart of Pope Francis
that he is symbolically represented on the *papal coat
of arms.* Next to the eight-pointed golden star, which
represents Our Lady in Catholic tradition, there appears
a gold spikenard flower, which represents St. Joseph (the
spikenard flower is sometimes seen in the hand of St.
Joseph in art and sculptures).

Saint Joseph was also represented on the coat of
arms of Bishop, and later Cardinal, Bergoglio when he
was in Argentina. So, going to Joseph is nothing new for
Pope Francis.

In another historic event, Pope Francis consecrated
the Vatican City State to the powerful intercession of St.

Joseph and St. Michael the Archangel on July 5, 2013. During the ceremony, the Holy Father stated:

> We also consecrate Vatican City to St. Joseph, the guardian of Jesus, the guardian of the Holy Family. May his presence make us even stronger and more courageous in giving space to God in our lives in order to always overcome evil with good.[77]

This tells us that Pope Francis's devotion to our spiritual father is something he believes to be critically important for the protection and the sanctification of the People of God *today, in our present moment of human history.*

It is crystal clear: the consistent line of contemporary popes, in faith, trust, and inspirational confidence, really do "go to Joseph" (Gen 41:55).

History also testifies to the fact that it was always fruitful for the Church and for the world when they have done so.

We close here with the words of Pope Francis, taken from his inaugural Mass as Pope on March 19, 2013, which he chose to celebrate on the solemnity of St. Joseph:

> How does Joseph respond to his calling to be the protector of Mary, Jesus and the Church? By being constantly attentive to God, open to the signs of God's presence and receptive to God's plans, and not simply to his own. This is what God asked of David, as we heard in the first reading. God does not want a house built by men, but faithfulness to his word, to his plan. It is God himself who builds the house, but from living stones sealed by his Spirit.

Joseph is a "protector" because he is able to hear God's voice and be guided by his will; and for this reason he is all the more sensitive to the persons entrusted to his safekeeping. He can look at things realistically, he is in touch with his surroundings, he can make truly wise decisions. In him, dear friends, we learn how to respond to God's call, readily and willingly, but we also see the core of the Christian vocation, which is Christ! Let us protect Christ in our lives, so that we can protect others, so that we can protect creation! ...

To protect Jesus with Mary, to protect the whole of creation, to protect each person, especially the poorest, to protect ourselves: This is a service that the Bishop of Rome is called to carry out, yet one to which all of us are called, so that the star of hope will shine brightly. Let us protect with love all that God has given us!

I implore the intercession of the Virgin Mary, Saint Joseph, Saints Peter and Paul, and Saint Francis, that the Holy Spirit may accompany my ministry, and I ask all of you to pray for me! Amen.[78]

Chapter 9

St. Joseph and Our Lady's Apparitions

It certainly sounds reasonable that where one spouse goes, the other spouse often follows.

We shouldn't be surprised, then, that in some of the most significant apparitions of Our Lady during our present universally designated "Age of Mary," there would be appearances from St. Joseph as well. While maintaining his biblical identity as the just and humble man of few words, when St. Joseph does appear or speak, it is of mammoth importance.

Knock, Ireland

As early as Our Lady's historic, though silent, apparition at Knock, Ireland, in 1879, St. Joseph appeared prominently.

On the night of August 21, 1879, the Irish visionary Mary Byrne saw Our Lady as a luminous figure, with St. Joseph on her right side. Saint Joseph had his head bowed to his wife in a gesture of reverence and respect. The visionary later described St. Joseph as not being as "white" as Our Lady, though himself luminous as well, and slightly older than she was.[79]

The third luminous figure at Knock was St. John the Evangelist, dressed as a bishop and in a posture of preaching. Saint John represents the Church and its hierarchy, of whom St. Joseph is Protector and Patron.

Saint Joseph's manifestation at this silent, Church-approved apparition tells us of the significance of St. Joseph in Our Lady's overall mission of bringing souls back to God through prayer, penance, conversion, and a return to the sacramental life of the Church.

Fatima, Portugal

During the great Marian apparitions of "Our Lady of the Rosary" at Fatima, Portugal, in 1917, St. Joseph again made a noteworthy appearance.

Her Fatima apparitions called the world to convert from sin, to pray the Rosary daily, to offer reparation to the Immaculate Heart of Mary, and to consecrate Russia to her Immaculate Heart. To do so would bring forth the "Triumph of her Immaculate Heart" — a historic release of grace for the Church and for the world that would eventually result in a period of global peace.

On October 13, 1917, Our Lady of the Rosary appeared for a sixth time in as many months and provided the 70,000 onlookers with the "Solar Miracle." This miracle of the sun was a sign of authenticity that she had foretold to the three Portuguese child visionaries earlier in the year.

The sun was described as "dancing" in the sky, giving off a series of different colors, and then dramatically racing toward the earth, only to then return to its position in the sky.

Right before the solar miracle took place, Our Lady appeared with St. Joseph at her side. He was holding the

Christ Child in his arms. At that moment, in a gesture packed with meaning, *St. Joseph and the Christ Child simultaneously blessed the world.*

What could this mean? Nothing short of the truth that St. Joseph's role as Patron and Protector of the Church at the service of Jesus and Mary will be key in initiating and fulfilling Fatima's promise for the Triumph of the Immaculate Heart of Mary.

In a nutshell: the Church will not triumph without the blessing and intercession of its official Guardian. (It should be noted here that St. Michael the Archangel is also considered a patron and protector of the Church, especially when it comes to spiritual warfare against Satan.)

Zeitoun, Egypt

A more contemporary series of apparitions that included St. Joseph (and which received approval from the rightful ecclesiastical authority) were the repeated appearances of St. Joseph, Our Lady, and the Child Jesus in the 1968 visions of the Holy Family in Zeitoun, Egypt.

Witnessed by thousands of Christian, Muslim, and Jewish pilgrims (as well as peoples of no faith at all), the Holy Family appeared over a Coptic Orthodox Church in this Egyptian suburb of Cairo. Cardinal Stephanos I (the Catholic Coptic Patriarch) stated that there can be "no doubt" that these were "true appearances" of the Boy Jesus (approximately 12 years old), Mary, and St. Joseph.[80]

We see again the powerful presence of St. Joseph, side by side with Jesus and Mary, as a celestial testimony to his importance in achieving the goal of their Two Hearts: the salvation and sanctification of souls today.

Our Lady of America

Another series of reported Marian apparitions that contain a truly profound body of messages regarding the life and role of our spiritual father are the reported messages of Our Lady of America.

Why are these reported messages worthy of our consideration? *Because the one who formerly served as the second highest canonical authority in the Church said they are.*

Cardinal Raymond Burke, formerly the prefect (head guy) of the Tribunal of Apostolic Signatura at the Vatican (the highest court of canon law in the Church) once wrote a letter to the United States Conference of Catholic Bishops in which he stated that on a canonical basis, the apparitions of Our Lady of America already have the status of an approved apparition.[81]

We are, therefore, on very solid ground in seeing at least as "worthy of examination" that which the former prefect of the highest court in the Church saw as already canonically approved.

Let's then take a look for ourselves at the Josephite revelations in the Our Lady of America apparitions, while at the same time being always ready to submit our beliefs to the definitive judgment of the Church.

The overall reported message from Our Lady of America[82] calls for prayer, conversion, consecration to Our Lady as the Immaculate Conception, and a special worldwide return to the virtue of purity through America. Our Lady has specifically asked for renewed teaching and preaching on the Divine Indwelling of the Trinity[83] in the hearts of those who love Jesus as a foundation for this requested renewal of Christian purity.

Most specifically, Our Lady has asked that a statue of her image as "Our Lady of America" be solemnly processed into the Basilica of the National Shrine of the Immaculate Conception in Washington, D.C., in the company of the United States bishops. This act of devotion, according to the messages, will release a great abundance of graces that will lead to countless spiritual "miracles of the heart," particularly (but not exclusively) in the area of Christian purity.[84]

Regarding our good St. Joseph, these messages actually confirm several of the best and greatest theories of Josephite theology proposed by Church Doctors and theologians over the centuries.

Let's look at some of the actual words reportedly revealed by St. Joseph himself regarding his earthly mission and its heavenly continuation on our behalf. I'm going to provide you with several of the complete messages regarding St. Joseph, since they are packed with theological meaning and fatherly example: two things that today's Christian fathers and families desperately need.

In October 1956, Sr. Mary Ephrem described the following locutions (or "words spoken") from the Just Man:

> In early October, 1956, about a week after Our Lady's first appearance, St. Joseph, though I did not see him at this time, spoke to me the following words:
>
> "It is true, my daughter, that immediately after my conception I was, through the future merits of Jesus and because of my exceptional role of future Virgin-Father, cleansed from the stain of original sin.
>
> I was from that moment confirmed in grace and never had the slightest stain on my soul. This is my unique privilege among men.

My pure heart also was from the first
moment of existence inflamed with love for God.
Immediately, at the moment when my soul was
cleansed from original sin, grace was infused into it
in such abundance that, excluding my holy spouse,
I surpassed the holiness of the highest angel in the
angelic choir. My heart suffered with the Hearts of
Jesus and Mary. Mine was a silent suffering, for it
was my special vocation to hide and shield, as long
as God willed, the Virgin Mother and Son from the
malice and hatred of men.

The most painful of my sorrows was that I knew
beforehand of their passion, yet would not be there
to console them.

Their future suffering was ever present to me
and became my daily cross, so I became, in union
with my holy spouse, co-redemptor of the human
race. Through compassion for the sufferings of
Jesus and Mary I co-operated, as no other, in the
salvation of the world.[85]

Already in this first message, we have some real
Josephite gems.

According to Sr. Mary Ephrem, St. Joseph reveals,
first of all, that he was preserved from original sin (similar
to being "baptized in the womb") one moment after his
conception, and then, from that time, he never committed
personal sin.

Now, keep in mind the principle that God gives the
graces necessary for each human being's vocation in life. Is
it surprising that the one whose vocation is to be the moral
father of Jesus and spouse of the Immaculate One would

receive the grace of pre-sanctification in the womb and the ongoing grace of keeping that sanctity preserved for the rest of his life?

Saint Joseph then speaks of his role as "co-redemptor" with Jesus and Mary of the human race.

Here, let's remember a couple of things. All Christians are called to be "co-redeemers in Christ," to use St. John Paul II's repeated expression.[86] All Christians, by their prayers, suffering, and acceptance of daily trials offered in union with the sufferings of Jesus and Mary, are called by St. Paul to "make up what is lacking in the sufferings of Christ" (Col 1:24). That is, as Christians, we all can cause a release of the infinite graces merited by Jesus Christ to be directed to souls in need, including to our own souls.

Saint Joseph is stating here that because he knew of the future sufferings of his virginal Son and wife and also knew that he would not be there when they would endure the greatest suffering in human history (a father's absolute nightmare!), he began to offer this pain throughout the rest of his life to such an efficacious degree that, after Jesus and Mary, St. Joseph was the greatest contributor to the victory of human salvation.

This speaks volumes about the power of human suffering when offered in union with the sufferings of Jesus and Mary for human salvation. This also speaks volumes about the purity and sanctity of St. Joseph's heart.

The next message truly amplifies the appropriateness of acknowledging St. Joseph's universal, spiritual fatherhood, and the critical need for the return of authentic fatherhood in our own time, as well as a revelation of the Just Man's "most pure heart." Thus, we read from Sr. Mary Ephrem's memoirs:

On March 11, 1958, Our Lady said to me: "Saint Joseph will come on the eve of his feast. Prepare yourself well. There will be a special message. My holy spouse has an important part to play in bringing peace to the world."

Saint Joseph came as was promised, and these are the words he spoke at this time: "Kneel down, my daughter, for what you will hear and what you will write will bring countless souls to a new way of life. Through you, small one, the Trinity desires to make known to souls Its desire to be adored, honored, and loved within the kingdom, the interior kingdom of their hearts. I bring to souls the purity of my life and the obedience that crowned it. All fatherhood is blest in me whom the Eternal Father chose as His representative on earth, the Virgin-Father of His own Divine Son. Through me the Heavenly Father has blessed all fatherhood, and through me He continues and will continue to do so till the end of time. My spiritual fatherhood extends to all God's children, and together with my Virgin Spouse I watch over them with great love and solicitude. Fathers must come to me, small one, to learn obedience to authority: to the Church always, as the mouthpiece of God, to the laws of the country in which they live, insofar as these do not go against God and their neighbor. Mine was perfect obedience to the Divine Will, as it was shown and made known to me by the Jewish law and religion. To be careless in this is most displeasing to God and will be severely punished in the next world. Let fathers also imitate my great purity of life and the deep respect I held for my Immaculate Spouse. Let them be an example to their children and fellowmen, never willfully doing anything that would cause scandal among God's people. Fatherhood is from God, and it must take once again its rightful place among men."

As St. Joseph ceased speaking I saw his most pure heart. It seemed to be lying on a cross which was of brown color. It appeared to me that at the top of the heart, in the midst of the flames pouring out, was a pure white lily. Then I heard these words:

"Behold this pure heart so pleasing to Him who made it."

Saint Joseph then continued:

"The cross, my little one, upon which my heart rests is the cross of the Passion, which was ever present before me, causing me intense suffering. I desire souls to come to my heart that they may learn true union with the Divine Will. It is enough, my child; I will come again tomorrow. Then I will make known to you how God wishes me to be honored in union with Jesus and Mary to obtain peace among men and nations. Good night, my little one."

In this second message, we receive not only a vivid description of Josephite fatherhood as the example par excellence for all fathers to emulate but also as a revelation of the saint's pure heart.

Note the power of the symbolism: his pure heart is *on a cross.*

Yes, the life of authentic Christian fatherhood is a life of suffering in service for the ones you love — your wife and your children — in all possible human circumstances. Authentic fatherhood cannot elude intense suffering for one's domestic Church. But it also brings forth graces of joy and happiness from one's precious family that constitute a true foretaste of heaven itself.

On March 19, 1958, the solemnity of St. Joseph, the saint spoke to the visionary about a feast that heaven desires to establish in honor of his "fatherhood." This request was immediately followed by a transcendent vision of our spiritual father:

> On the evening of the next day, March 19, 1958, St. Joseph again appeared to me as he had promised and addressed me in these words:
> "My child, I desire a day to be set aside to honor my fatherhood. The privilege of being chosen by God to be the Virgin-Father of His Son was mine alone, and no honor, excluding that bestowed upon my Holy Spouse, was ever, or will ever, be as sublime or as high as this. The Holy Trinity desires thus to honor me that in my unique fatherhood all fatherhood might be blessed. Dear child, I was king in the little home of Nazareth, for I sheltered within it the Prince of Peace and the Queen of Heaven. To me they looked for protection and sustenance, and I did not fail them. I received from them the deepest love and reverence, for in me they saw Him whose place I took over them. So the head of the family must be loved, obeyed, and respected, and in return be a true father and protector to those under his care. In honoring in a special way my fatherhood, you also honor Jesus and Mary. The Divine Trinity

has placed into our keeping the peace of the world.
The imitation of the Holy Family, my child, and
of the virtues we practiced in our little home at
Nazareth is the way for all souls to that peace
which comes from God alone and which none
other can give."

Then suddenly, as he ceased speaking, I was
favored with a unique and marvelous vision of
the glorious St. Joseph. He seemed suspended,
as it were, a short distance above what had the
appearance of a large globe with clouds moving
about it. His head was slightly raised, the eyes
gazing upward as if in ecstasy. The hands were in
a position similar to that of the priest during the
celebration of Holy Mass, only they extended
upward somewhat. The color of his hair, as also of
his rather small and slightly forked beard, seemed
a very dark brown. His eyes resembled in color the
hair and beard. He was clothed in a white robe that
reached to his ankles. Over this he wore a sort of
cloak which did not come together at the throat,
but covering the shoulders and draped gracefully
over each arm, reached to the hem of the robe.
The cloak at times had, or seemed to have, the
appearance of a brown, sometimes a purple, hue, or
perhaps a slight blending of the two. The belt about
his waist was of a gold color, as were his sandals.
His appearance, though quite youthful, gave at the
same time the impression of rare maturity combined
with great strength. He seemed a bit taller than
medium height. The lines of his face appeared
strong and purposeful, softened somewhat by a

gentle serenity. I also saw his most pure heart at this time. Moreover, I saw the Holy Spirit in the form of a dove hovering above his head. Standing sideways, facing each other, were two angels, one on the right, the other on the left. Each carried what appeared to be a small pillow in a satin covering, the pillow on the right bearing a gold crown, the one on the left, a gold scepter. The angels were all white, even their faces and hair. It was a beautiful whiteness that reminded me of the stainlessness of heaven. Then I heard these words:

"Thus should he be honored whom the King desires to honor."

When the vision ended, St. Joseph before taking leave spoke to me in the following manner:

"The Holy Father need have no fear, for I have been appointed his special protector. As God chose me to be the special guardian of His Son, so has He chosen me as the special guardian of him who in Christ's Name is head of the Mystical Body of that same Son on earth. My special protection of the Holy Father and the Church should be made known to him. God wishes to make this known to him that he may receive thereby renewed consolation and encouragement. During the war, little daughter, it was I who saved him from death at the hands of his enemies. Continually I watch over him and the Church, and I desire this to be acknowledged for the greater glory of God and the good of souls. Lovely child, precious to the heart of your spiritual father, I will come again on the last Sunday of this month. Jesus and Mary will come also in a special visit. Receive my blessing."

As I knelt down to receive it, I felt his hands on my head and heard the words: "May Jesus and Mary through my hands bestow upon you eternal peace."[87]

With this feast, we would celebrate the best human father of all time, and encourage in all other human fathers the spiritual and domestic incentive to follow his example.

Finally, in this March 30, 1958, message, St. Joseph confirms his role as the Church's Protector and calls for a "First Wednesday" devotion to his "Pure Heart." As he had promised, St. Joseph came again on March 30. His requests were similar to those of Our Lady of Fatima and the First Saturday devotion. The Sacred Hearts of Jesus, Mary, and Joseph have been chosen by the Most Holy Trinity to bring peace to the world; hence, their request for special love and honor, also, in particular, for reparation and imitation. These are the words of St. Joseph as recorded on March 30:

"I am the protector of the Church and the home, as I was the protector of Christ and His Mother while I lived upon earth. Jesus and Mary desire that my pure heart, so long hidden and unknown, be now honored in a special way. Let my children honor my most pure heart in a special manner on the First Wednesday of the month by reciting the Joyful Mysteries of the Rosary in memory of my life with Jesus and Mary and the love I bore them, the sorrow I suffered with them. Let them receive Holy Communion in union with the love with which I received the Savior for the first time and each time I held Him in my arms. Those who honor me in this way will be consoled by my presence at their death, and I myself will conduct them safely into the presence of Jesus and Mary. I will come again, little child of my most pure heart. Until then, continue in patience and humility, which is so pleasing to God."

As St. Joseph had promised, Jesus and Mary also came on March 30. Jesus had the appearance of a boy about 15 or 16 years old. He spoke to me first. It was about the sanctification of the family and other matters. He said it would not be required of me to write it at this time, as He would ask this of me at a later date. Our Lady and St. Joseph also spoke to me concerning the same subject and also about the Divine Indwelling.

Our "protector of the Church and home" makes a powerful promise with his request for devotion on the first Wednesdays of each month in the form of: 1) praying the Joyful Mysteries of the Rosary while pondering the life, love, and sorrow of the Just Man with Jesus and Our Lady; 2) and receiving Holy Communion, united with the love with which St. Joseph received the Infant Jesus for the first time.

For these two acts of devotion on our part every first Wednesday, St. Joseph reportedly promises on his part to console us with his presence at our death and to personally lead our souls into the presence of Jesus and Mary. Now that's one great exchange.

One thing is clear about these reported messages of St. Joseph, as well as the other visits of the Just Man in approved Marian apparitions: St. Joseph, as the Church's

Protector and as our personal spiritual father, has a quintessential role in the serious and mounting struggle against sin, godlessness, and the seemingly ever-present, tragic rejection, not only of divine revelation, but also of the Natural Law written by God into human hearts.

The Church in general and each one of us in particular are in the midst of an unprecedented spiritual war. Thank God that we have been given the same protector and guardian Jesus himself had during his childhood and young adulthood to see us through, safely and victoriously.

Now is the time to call upon our spiritual father and protector.

Chapter 10

You, St. Joseph, and All of Us

Now that you're knowledgeable about the basic biblical, traditional, patristic, medieval, contemporary, and papal aspects of Josephite devotion, as well as what private revelations tell us about St. Joseph — now what?

Venerable Fulton Sheen used to say at the end of his inspired priest retreats that if, after all the facts, insights, and anecdotes, the retreatants did not commit to do a daily Holy Hour before the Blessed Sacrament, then the retreat had been a failure.

I would say the same about this concise work on St. Joseph: If, after knowing all you have gleaned from these facts, insights, and anecdotes about St. Joseph, it does not lead you *to a greater love and devotion to your spiritual father*, then this book has likewise been a failure.

But I'm confident that it hasn't been because of two factors: 1) St. Joseph's goodness and 2) your goodness. That's a great combination for a long lasting and efficacious friendship.

That's what authentic Christian devotion really is at its core: a spiritual friendship between two members of the Mystical Body that leads to greater holiness and deeper love.

That's why the first aspect of true devotion to St. Joseph focuses on *you*.

There's no such thing as a unilateral or "one-sided" friendship. You have to respond to God's invitation for you through his Church to have a special relationship with the virginal father of Jesus, the husband of Mary, and your own spiritual father. It's ultimately your decision as to how and what kind of relationship you want with the holiest man who ever walked the earth (except, of course, Jesus who is both God and man) and who seeks to guard and protect you from his heavenly vantage point — *if you let him.*

But he can only guard and protect you to the extent that you give him your "yes." The Heavenly Father is very protective of his greatest gift to you — your freedom — and not even St. Joseph can force his help upon you, no matter how much he desires to assist you in both the spiritual and temporal realms. So, your relationship with St. Joseph is ultimately up to you.

Now, the second part of true devotion to the Just Man focuses on "all of *us*."

That's right. Your devotion to St. Joseph, no matter how deep and intimate, is never something entirely exclusive. It always includes the dimension of the entire Church — the body of believers in Jesus, which includes the saints in heaven, the celestial choirs of angels, the Holy Souls in Purgatory, and the People of God on earth. In other words, authentic devotion to St. Joseph not only unites you more closely to the Hearts of Jesus and Mary, as well as to his own pure heart, but it also unites you to the hearts of everyone else in the family we call "the Church." And that's what good parents do so well. They don't just keep their love to themselves but spread it throughout the entire family, so each family member experiences the love of the family as a whole.

To experience the love of as many faith-filled members of the Church as possible is to experience the beginnings of heaven. This is just one more sublime fruit of devotion to our spiritual father.

So let's look at five major ways we can foster our devotion to St. Joseph — ways that traditionally have been very successful in improving our relationship with the Just Man.

The Litany of St. Joseph

From medieval times, the frequent recital of the Litany of St. Joseph has been a cherished method of coming to know the saint and love him more. By prayerfully repeating his most celebrated titles, while at the same time asking for his intercession under each title, we are more intimately united to this great saint. For, indeed, each title is packed with meaning about St. Joseph's life, mission, and powerful protection.

From the title "Mirror of Patience" (great for dads to remember!) to "Glory of Home Life" (for more dedication to our families) to the powerful "Terror of Demons" (St. Joseph's intercession gives us spiritual protection against the attacks of Satan), the Litany constitutes a great summary of the Christian virtues that each Christian should daily imitate and, at the same time, it invokes St. Joseph's never-failing intercession.

During my oldest son's wedding, at which I was blessed to preside as a deacon, my homily message to him was to daily recite the Litany of St. Joseph as a powerful aid in his efforts to live as a good Christian husband and father.

I would humbly offer the same counsel to every husband and father — not exclusively to fathers, but certainly to fathers! — as something like a daily examination of domestic conscience. Through the praying of the Litany, we can gauge how we're doing each day as Christian husbands and fathers in light of the *finest example* for Christian husbands and fathers.

(You can find the complete Litany of St. Joseph in Appendix Two.)

The Seven Joys and Sorrows of St. Joseph

Typically, when one first hears of the Seven Joys and Sorrows of St. Joseph, he is told the story of two priests sailing in a ship carrying hundreds of passengers off the coast of Flanders. The ship suddenly experiences a great storm and is destroyed, and most of the passengers are lost. The two priests hold on to a plank for several days and nights, while constantly calling upon the intercession of St. Joseph for help. On the third day, a man appears to them in a vision and guides them to safe harbor. Upon being asked by the two grateful priests his identity, he reveals that he is St. Joseph and asks them to recite daily the "Our Father" and "Hail Mary" seven times, each time meditating upon the seven joys and sorrows of his life.

These seven biblically founded events, which at the same time possess aspects of true joy and true suffering for St. Joseph, are as follows:

1. The doubt of St. Joseph (Mt 1:19) and the Message of the Angel (Mt 1:20).
2. The poverty of Jesus' birth (Lk 2:7) and the birth itself (Lk 2:7).

3. The Circumcision (Lk 2:21) and the Holy Name of Jesus (Mt 1:25).
4. The prophecy of Simeon that many would be lost (Lk 2:34) and his prophecy that many would rise (Lk 2:34)
5. The flight into Egypt (Mt 2:14) and the overthrow of idols (Is 19:1).
6. The return from Egypt (Mt 2:22) and life with Mary and Jesus (Lk 2:39).
7. The losing of the Child Jesus (Lk 2:45) and the finding of the Child Jesus in the Temple (Lk 2:46).

The Seven Joys and Sorrows illustrate another simple principle: the more we prayerfully ponder St. Joseph's life, the more we sanctify our own lives.

(A traditionally structured prayer version of the Seven Joys and Sorrows can be found in Appendix Two.)

The Cord of St. Joseph

The Cord (or Cincture) of St. Joseph can be traced back to 1657. An Augustinian nun in Antwerp, Belgium, was experiencing excruciating pain for several years and, at the point of death, petitioned St. Joseph for a cure. During this same time, she took a cord, had it blessed in St. Joseph's honor, and wrapped it around herself. She then went before a statue of St. Joseph, pleaded for his intercession, and she immediately was freed from all pain. Her physician, a Protestant Christian, declared her healing to be a miracle.

The practice of wearing the cord spread, and by the 19th century, Pope Leo XIII approved confraternities of the Cord of St. Joseph and granted indulgences for wearing the cord and participating in the other prayers of the Confraternity.

It is also a common practice for those not associated with a confraternity to simply wear the cord in honor of St. Joseph and to petition the graces of St. Joseph's special protection in the following areas: the virtue of chastity; final perseverance in being true to our faith until death; and invoking St. Joseph's assistance at the hour of death. (Because St. Joseph has the title "Patron of a Happy Death" — by virtue of his own death in the arms of Jesus and Mary — it only makes sense that he would grant similar graces to us at the hour of our death upon our request.)

The actual cord, a thread made out of cotton, typically comes with one knot tied at each end, and then you tie another five knots into the cord. These seven knots represents the Seven Joys and Sorrows of St. Joseph. The cord can be blessed by a priest or deacon and is then worn around the waist.

One common practice is to say a "Glory Be" each day for each one of the seven knots while meditating on the Seven Joys and Sorrows.

The Cord of St. Joseph can be a great sacramental and spiritual remedy for those who are caught in the rampant impurity and immodesty of contemporary society.

Memorare to St. Joseph

The Memorare to St. Joseph is another very popular prayer. It is sometimes used to invoke the immediate intercession of St. Joseph for times when the prayer intention can't wait for a full novena of nine days.

A quick, easy, yet powerful prayer, the Memorare to St. Joseph is sometimes prayed nine times in a row as a kind of "short-cut" novena invoking the great saint's intercession as soon as possible.

Referring to the famous testimony of St. Teresa of Avila that with St. Joseph "never hath it been heard that anyone who has invoked thy protection or sought thy mediation has not obtained relief," this powerful, little prayer of petition goes on to invoke St. Joseph, asking him to grant the requested petition.

(You can find two versions of the Memorare to St. Joseph in Appendix Two.)

Act of Consecration to St. Joseph

Finally, we come to what many consider the highpoint, summit, and climax of devotion to St. Joseph: the act of consecration to our spiritual father. But before we look at consecrating ourselves to St. Joseph, we should first examine the question: What exactly is an act of consecration to a saint?

Consecration to Saints in General

An act of consecration to a saint is to make a gift of self and a promise of love by which we give our "yes" to receiving the greatest possible intercession that the saint has to offer. In this way, we are giving the saint our consent to be more closely united to him or her and also to receiving the fullest possible intercession the saint can offer to us. This is something approved by the Church as evidenced, for instance, by the recent Vatican approval of making a personal consecration to one's guardian angel.[88]

Now, at this point, it is very important to note that any act of consecration — of giving ourselves over to a saint's intercession and receiving all that the saint has to offer — ultimately goes to God through the saint. Moreover, it is God himself who has granted a saint the power of intercession by virtue of the saint's excellence in loving God during his or her earthly life. So, all the devotion and love we offer to a saint ultimately praises the object of his or her love, which is God himself. This is why we can rightly say, as does the Church down through the centuries, that to honor the saints is ultimately to give glory to God.

The Two Highest Forms of Saint-consecration

The highest form of consecration to a saint is that involving she who is the highest of all saints: Mary. When a person consecrates himself to the Mother of God, he grants her his permission to fully intercede on his behalf by virtue of her heavenly mission of uniting all her earthly children with her first Child. And this is something we should never underestimate: namely, *the power of Our Lady's full-blown intercession!*

Something else we should not underestimate is the strength of St. Joseph's powerful intercession. Even though St. Joseph is not the Mediatrix of all graces as is his holy spouse, he nevertheless possesses the second greatest human power of intercession in the Mystical Body (as you are well aware of at this point in the book). Therefore, consecrating oneself to St. Joseph is extremely efficacious for one's spiritual growth.

Still, people might say, "I thought you could only consecrate yourself to God and Mary?" People may say this because, thanks be to God, Marian consecration has become very popular these days. Nevertheless, we can and should also consecrate ourselves to St. Joseph — even before consecrating ourselves to other saints. For, while it is a good and pious act to consecrate oneself to other saints, consecration to St. Joseph has pride of place, after Marian consecration. One reason for this is that Marian consecration and the consecration to St. Joseph go hand in hand, which is based on the mystery of the Holy Family.

When we reflect on the Holy Family of Jesus, Mary, and Joseph, we come to realize that Jesus Christ was the first one to entrust (consecrate) himself to Mary and Joseph, the first to put himself under their special care and protection. Well, shouldn't we do the same? Aren't we called to imitate Jesus? Aren't Mary and Joseph our parents, too? Of course! So, because of all this, because Jesus put himself under Joseph and Mary's special care, because we're called to imitate Christ, and because Mary and Joseph are our parents, too, we're invited to consecrate ourselves to Mary and Joseph and be more fully a part of the Holy Family. In short, we're invited to the most perfect imitation of Christ.

The Church herself seems to have recognized the importance of putting herself under St. Joseph's special care and protection by declaring St. Joseph as the Universal Patron of the Church. Also, the Church herself has historically appreciated several forms of consecration directly to St. Joseph, which are to be recommended to the faithful. In the next section, I'll recommend two specific forms of consecration to St. Joseph.

Two Forms of Consecration to St. Joseph

When we give St. Joseph our "yes" to use his unrestricted power of fatherly intercession and protection on our behalf, this results in nothing less than a huge increase of grace and blessing for each one of us who, in this formal and definitive way, accept him as our spiritual father.

God has also given St. Joseph some specific areas where his intercession is particularly powerful: for family protection, purity, financial help, one's job or work, a happy death, and on and on. Consecration to St. Joseph provides for strong intercession in these particular areas of human need. For a simple, easy-to-make nine-day consecration that highlights the various areas of St. Joseph's powerful intercession, you may be interested in using the excellent preparation for consecration found in Appendix One written by Fr. Michael Gaitley, MIC, author of the very popular preparatory guide for Marian consecration *33 Days to Morning Glory.*

I've composed another, very flexible form of consecration, which you can find at the end of this chapter. I'm recommending either Fr. Gaitley's or my format, so you'll have no excuse *not* to make the consecration. And why not use them both?

Here's how you can make the consecration I've composed. First, perhaps you could determine a reasonable period of time, whether it be seven days (in honor of St. Joseph's Seven Joys and Sorrows), nine days (something more like a novena) or even, if preferable, 33 days (like the 33 days of preparation for Marian Consecration), during which you could in a special way prepare for your consecration to St. Joseph.

It could also be meaningful (as well as serve as a helpful reminder in the future for eventually renewing your consecration) to pick a day of "Josephite significance." This could be, for example, the first Wednesday of any given month, a feast honoring St. Joseph, a feast honoring the Holy Family, or even a great Marian feast in light of Our Lady's great unity with St. Joseph. You could count back 7, 9, or 33 days, for example, and determine to do a brief series of prayers daily that lead up to that designated day of consecration.

What prayers could you pray? It's entirely up to you. You may choose to pray the Joyful Mysteries of the Rosary while meditating on St. Joseph's life and virtues as daily preparation leading up to the big day. Or you may add praying the Litany of Saint Joseph, or possibly the Seven Joys and Sorrows Prayer as well on each day of your preparation. You may have time to do the Joyful Mysteries, the Litany, and the Seven Joys and Sorrows Prayer for an excellent preparation, or you may feel like it's only realistic to pray one of these Josephite prayers.

At this point, I invite you to sincerely ask your spiritual father to guide you to the best and most realistic preparation for you in making a meaningful consecration. Ask him to direct you to the best practical means by which you can personally and faithfully "go to Joseph."

In conclusion, then, my deepest prayer and hope for you is that through this short journey to the Just Man, by knowing him better, you are growing to love him more.

You will never regret making room in your heart for the pure heart of Joseph. He will lead you into the most mystical depths of the most loving Hearts of Jesus and Mary, while at the same time helping you in the most practical necessities of your earthly life — and all the while remaining the humble, gentle, fatherly protector of you and your loved ones.

May you always peacefully, trustingly, joyfully "go to Joseph" (Gen 44:15).

Act of Consecration to St. Joseph

Heavenly Father, you gave to St. Joseph, by the power of the Holy Spirit, the graces and virtues necessary to be a virginal father to your Son, Our Lord, Jesus Christ. Grant us now the grace and humility to imitate his holy virtues, and to receive fully his powerful intercession.

Lord Jesus, who St. Joseph was to you during your earthly life, St. Joseph is to us as members of your Body. Help us to honor your earthly father as our own spiritual father, in imitation of you.

Holy Mother Mary, St. Joseph was united to you as husband through the holy bond of matrimony. Grant us the grace, as Mediatrix of all graces, to give ourselves entirely without reserve to your most chaste husband for our own purity, protection, and the fulfillment of our vocation of Christian life.

Saint Joseph, you are the virginal father of Jesus Christ, the spouse of Mary Immaculate, the Patron of the Universal Church, and the holiest man who ever lived. Today, I (name) consecrate myself to you without reserve. I give myself to you, I place myself under your most powerful protection, and I ask you to do for me what you did for Jesus and Mary in perpetual spiritual and temporal protection. I ask you to use the full power of your intercession to help me to be always faithful to my baptismal promises to Jesus, my Lord and Savior; to be loving to Mary, my spiritual mother; and to be obedient to our Holy Father, the Pope, of whom you are special protector. Today, good St. Joseph, I formally accept you as my spiritual father. May I grow in your virtues, O greatest of Patriarchs, and receive with an open heart your spiritual help and protection for me personally and for the entire Church of Jesus Christ.

I entrust myself entirely to you, my spiritual father, and I praise God for the gift you are to me, to the Church, and to the world. Saint Joseph, I give myself to you, and I love you. Amen.

Appendices

Nine Days to Joseph
A Preparation for Consecration

I just sat down to write this preparation for consecration to St. Joseph and realized an amazing coincidence: *Today is my last day as "Fr. Joseph, MIC."*

That title, "Fr. Joseph," is an honorary designation for the grueling office job I've held for the last three-and-a-half years, namely, the director of the Association of Marian Helpers. I say "grueling" because ... well, let me put it this way: Shortly before my priestly ordination, my provincial superior called me into his office and said, "Brother Michael, how would you feel about being the next Fr. Joseph?" I replied, "What's that?" He continued, "Well, if I told you, you'd say no. ... *So just say yes.*"

Now I know what he meant! The job was *not* easy — but thankfully, St. Joseph helped me in a big way, a way that's related to the preparation for consecration you're about to read. Let me tell you what happened.

After two years on the job as "Fr. Joseph," I was feeling broken down and burned out. I spoke with my superior to see if another priest could fill the position or come help me in the office. Unfortunately, nobody was available, at least not for another year. So, with my health declining, spirit failing, and the work piling up, a hopeful thought suddenly occurred to me on the solemnity of St. Joseph: "Give it all to Joseph. He'll take care of it."

I knew exactly what to do. I got on my computer and typed out a consecration or "entrustment" to St. Joseph. I brought it to Mass at the office where I worked, and following Mass, I solemnly and publicly put everything — myself, my staff, the office, and our work — into the strong, caring hands of St. Joseph. And then, all *heaven* broke loose. Let me just say that from our Marian Helpers Center in Stockbridge, Massachusetts, our evangelization works rapidly multiplied, and we were able to bring the message of God's mercy and devotion to Mary to millions more people. Looking back now on that day of entrustment, I firmly believe that St. Joseph was behind this new and dramatic growth.

So, in gratitude to St. Joseph, on this my last day as "Fr. Joseph," I'm writing this brief, heartfelt preparation for consecrating oneself to St. Joseph. I say "brief" because St. Joseph was a man of few words — not one of them is recorded in Scripture! — and my guess is that he probably appreciates brevity. I say "heartfelt" because this preparation really comes from my heart, especially as I look back and clearly see how St. Joseph came through for me during my time of need as "Fr. Joseph." But before we get to these "nine days to Joseph," let me briefly explain how this preparation works.

Basically, you pray the specified prayer to St. Joseph each day from the heart for nine days. Then, on the last day (the 10th day), the Day of Consecration, you'll pray the prayer of consecration from the heart. It's that simple.

Of course, you'll probably want to time the days so the Day of Consecration falls on a feast of St. Joseph (either March 19, May 1, or the feast of the Holy Family) or on a Marian feast (because of St. Joseph's closeness to Mary). I also recommend that on the day of your consecration, you write it out in your own handwriting, date it, and then renew it each year. And by the way, this is a perfect complement to Marian consecration, because of St. Joseph's closeness to and love for Mary.

Day One — *St. Joseph, Powerful Intercessor*

Dear St. Joseph,

After Mary, you're the most powerful intercessor before God. In a sense, Jesus remains obedient to you and will listen to you as you bring my intentions to him. Because of this, I especially want to entrust myself to your fatherly care, just as Jesus himself did. And while in the past, I may have brought to you one of my intentions here or there, this time I want to do something new. This time, I want to give you *all*. In other words, St. Joseph, I'm not here to offer you a regular "novena" for just one of my intentions. Rather, I want to forever entrust to you *all* of my needs and cares, trusting that you will bring them, with Mary, to your Son, Jesus.

Dear St. Joseph, as the best of fathers, as the one God chose to be the virginal father of Jesus, I believe that you know what I need better than I do myself. So, go ahead, St. Joseph. I give you permission to care for me as your child. In doing so, I trust that you will do everything in your power to make my life into something beautiful for God. I trust that you will watch over me and that your prayers will guide me, bless me, and protect me. I trust that you will now care for me with the same love and tenderness with which you cared for Jesus. I'll confirm this special relationship with you in nine days, when I make my prayer of consecration.

Saint Joseph, Powerful Intercessor, please pray for me and all my intentions.

Day Two — St. Joseph, Loving Spouse of Mary

Dear St. Joseph,

I'm thinking about the angel's words to you, "Do not be afraid to take Mary for your wife" (Mt 1:20). Saint Joseph, you weren't afraid. You trusted God. And now you truly are the husband of Mary. After Jesus, you are the dearest human person to her heart! Well, St. Joseph, as my spiritual father, I now ask you to speak to Mary about me, about my life. If you kindly adopt me as your spiritual child, then I know all the more that Mary will take me to her heart as well. Both of you truly are my spiritual parents. And just as any good father wants to see his children love their mother, I know that you will help me to know and love my spiritual mother more. By your powerful prayers, I ask you to help me realize what a gift I have in Mary. Pray for me that I will better appreciate her motherly role in my life. Saint Joseph, I know that you love her. I know it makes you happy to see her children love her with all their hearts. Therefore, as I prepare to consecrate myself totally to your fatherly care, I give you permission — in fact, I'm pleading with you: Help me to appreciate my Mother Mary even more.

Saint Joseph, Loving Spouse of Mary, please help me to love my spiritual mother even more.

Day Three — St. Joseph, Good Provider

Dear St. Joseph,

As the foster father of Jesus, you provided for his human needs. Through the work of your hands, he had food to strengthen him, a house to give him shelter, and clothes to keep him warm. Now, from heaven, you're still working, St. Joseph. Indeed, the loving labor of your prayers provide for all the members of the Body of your Son. But as I'm preparing to consecrate myself completely to you, I ask you to please provide for me and for my loved ones in a special way. Through your prayers, please make sure that we always have food to eat, a roof over our heads, and clothes to wear. Also, please pray for us that in times of abundance, we will never forget God. Pray for us that we will always be grateful for God's gifts and that we will never be slaves to things like food or money, pleasure or power. Finally, help us always to remember and be generous with the poor.

Saint Joseph, with you as my spiritual father, I will do my best not to give in to useless anxiety about my job, money, or material things. I believe you will always make sure I have what I need, and as a good father, I ask that you indulge me a bit by even providing for my material wants, provided they don't take me away from Jesus.

Saint Joseph, Good Provider, please provide for my needs through your powerful prayers.

Day Four — St. Joseph, Strong Guardian

Dear St. Joseph,

When I think that God gave me my guardian angel and St. Michael to daily watch over me and defend me, I'm not afraid. But then, when I think that you, who are even more powerful before God, are my spiritual father, when I think that you are the "Terror of Demons," when I think of how you protected the Baby Jesus from Herod, then I am completely at peace (or, at least, I know I should be).

Saint Joseph, please pray that I will have the peace that comes from trusting in your fatherly protection. Saint Joseph, I believe that you will protect me from my enemies, seen and unseen. I believe that you will protect me from bodily and spiritual harm. I trust in your fatherly care. Saint Joseph, I will do my best not to give in to fear, knowing that you are praying for me in a special way as a child who has formally consecrated himself to your fatherly care.

Saint Joseph, Strong Guardian, please defend me with your prayers.

Day Five — St. Joseph, Who Did God's Will

Dear St. Joseph,

You did God's will. Dare I say you did it perfectly? Saint Joseph, I want to also do God's most perfect will. But on my own, I will fail. I need your help. I trust that with you as my spiritual father, you will guide me to always do God's most perfect will. Truly, St. Joseph, I want to reach the degree of glory that God has prepared for me in heaven. I want to bear fruit that will last. I don't want to let God down. I want to be a saint. Help me, St. Joseph. You see how weak and sinful I am. But teach me, good father. Help me to follow the commandments and please make my heart sensitive to the inspirations of the Holy Spirit. I know that as I entrust myself to your care, you will guide me and show me how to always do God's will. I give you permission to redirect the stream of my life if it ever departs from God's most perfect will.

Saint Joseph, who did God's will, please always keep me in God's most perfect will.

Day Six — St. Joseph, Who Suffered with Love

Dear St. Joseph,

As the day draws closer when I will consecrate myself to you, I can't help but notice how you suffered with love. You suffered darkness and confusion when Mary was found with child. You suffered the sacrifice of your flesh as you lovingly offered up the absence of bodily intimacy in marriage. You suffered a sword in your heart with Mary when Simeon foretold the passion of your Son. You suffered stress and uncertainty when you had to escape with your family to Egypt and live as an immigrant. You suffered crushing anxiety when your 12-year-old Son was lost for three days. You daily suffered fatigue and bodily aches from your manual labor. Worst of all, your fatherly heart grieved at knowing that you could not be there for Jesus and Mary when their darkest hour would one day come.

Saint Joseph, thank you for what you suffered in God's service, in union with your Son, for my salvation. I love you, St. Joseph. Thank you for your yes. Now, please help me to suffer with love as you did. When I suffer, help me not to complain. Help me not to forget to love. Help me not to forget others. Dear St. Joseph, through my suffering, watch over my poor heart: May it not harden but rather become more merciful. Help me to remember all God's children who are suffering in the world, and help me to offer my suffering for them and for the good of the Church. I am counting on you, St. Joseph. I know you will be with me, helping me to suffer with love.

Saint Joseph, who suffered with love, please help me also to suffer with a love like yours.

Day Seven — St. Joseph, Pure of Heart

Dear St. Joseph,

I said I want to be a saint, and saints need to be pure not only of body but of soul. Regarding purity of body, St. Joseph, guard me, protect me, and defend me from temptations against purity. I rely on you, St. Joseph. Don't let me fall. Don't let my eyes or thoughts wander. If they do, please bring them back to Jesus. I trust in you, St. Joseph. You lived purely with Mary in the midst of her beauty. Help me to see the beauty of others with your own pure vision. If I fall, help me to find God's mercy and free me from any bondage to such sin. Regarding purity of intentions, help me do everything not to please myself or others but to please God alone. Give me this grace as my dear spiritual father. I trust in you, St. Joseph.

Saint Joseph, Pure of Heart, please lend me your own purity of heart.

Day Eight — St. Joseph, Man of Peace and Joy

Dear St. Joseph,

I know the Bible doesn't speak directly of your joy, but how could you not have been full of joy? I'm sure you were. You lived in the presence of Jesus and Mary. Well, St. Joseph, please pray for me that I will also find my joy by living in their presence. And having yourself lived in their presence, you must have been a man of such peace. St. Joseph, please pray for me that I keep my joy and not give in to sadness, laziness, or discouragement. Also, pray that I keep my peace of soul and not hold on to anger and bitterness in my heart. Help me to be merciful to everyone by offering forgiveness that I might also, like you, be a man of true peace and joy.

Saint Joseph, Man of Peace and Joy, please put me at peace and help me find joy.

Day Nine — St. Joseph, Who Died So Beautifully

Dear St. Joseph,

I know I am going to die. When I do, I trust that you will be there to greet me with Jesus and Mary in a special way. Will you please promise me this? I trust you. I believe that you will be there for me. For my part, I will try not to be afraid of my death, and I will live my life in preparation for it. I will maybe even look forward to it as the time when I will get to meet you face to face. Prepare me for my death, whenever it may be. If it is sudden, please make sure that my soul is prepared and please make sure I will not be lost! Dear St. Joseph, obtain this grace for me as I consecrate myself to your fatherly care. Tomorrow, I am fully yours. Someday I will die, and I give you permission to take me home to my Father's house when that day comes.

Saint Joseph, who died so beautifully, please prepare my soul for death.

Day of Consecration to St. Joseph

Dear St. Joseph,

On this day, before God and your Immaculate Spouse, Mary, I, _____ , choose you as my spiritual father forever. I formally entrust myself to your paternal care. I love you, and I trust in your prayers for my life. As your spiritual child, I give you full permission (and in fact, I'm begging you) to please act in my life, especially by ...

Praying for me constantly in a special way,
Bringing me even deeper into the Hearts of Jesus
    and Mary,
Providing for me and all my loved ones,
Guarding and protecting me from bodily and
    spiritual evil,
Guiding me to always do God's most perfect will,
Helping me to suffer with love and without
    complaint,
Giving me purity of body and of soul,
Forming me into a person of peace and joy, and
Preparing me for a beautiful and happy death.

From this day forward, St. Joseph, you are my spiritual father, and I am your child. I trust you and love you, and I look forward to meeting you someday in heaven. I ask all of this in Jesus' name and for the glory of God, who is Father, Son, and Holy Spirit. Amen.

Devotional Prayers to St. Joseph

The Litany of St. Joseph

Lord, *have mercy on us.*
Christ, *have mercy on us.*
Lord, *have mercy on us.*

Christ, *hear us.*
Christ, *graciously hear us.*

God the Father of Heaven,
    Have mercy on us.
God the Son, Redeemer of the world,
    Have mercy on us.
God the Holy Spirit,
    Have mercy on us.

Holy Trinity, One God,
    Have mercy on us.

Holy Mary,
    Pray for us.

St. Joseph,
Pray for us.
Renowned offspring of David,
Pray for us.
Light of Patriarchs,
Pray for us.
Spouse of the Mother of God,
Pray for us.
Chaste guardian of the Virgin,
Pray for us.
Foster father of the Son of God,
Pray for us.
Diligent protector of Christ,
Pray for us.
Head of the Holy Family,
Pray for us.
Joseph most just,
Pray for us.
Joseph most chaste,
Pray for us.
Joseph most prudent,
Pray for us.
Joseph most strong,
Pray for us.
Joseph most obedient,
Pray for us.
Joseph most faithful,
Pray for us.
Mirror of patience,
Pray for us.
Lover of poverty,
Pray for us.

Model of artisans,
   Pray for us.
Glory of home life,
   Pray for us.
Guardian of virgins,
   Pray for us.
Pillar of families,
   Pray for us.
Solace of the wretched,
   Pray for us.
Hope of the sick,
   Pray for us.
Patron of the dying,
   Pray for us.
Terror of demons,
   Pray for us.
Protector of Holy Church,
   Pray for us.

Lamb of God, You who take away the sins of the world,
   spare us, O Lord!
Lamb of God, You who take away the sins of the world,
   graciously hear us, O Lord!
Lamb of God, You who take away the sins of the world,
   have mercy on us.

   V.   He made him the lord of His household.

   R.   *And prince over all His possessions.*

Let us pray:

*O God, who in Your ineffable providence did vouchsafe to
choose Blessed Joseph to be the spouse of Your most holy Mother;*

grant, we beseech You, that we may be worthy to have him for our intercessor in heaven whom on earth we venerate as our Protector. Amen.

The Seven Sorrows and Seven Joys of St. Joseph

The Seven Sorrows of St. Joseph

1. The Doubts of St. Joseph
2. The Poverty of Jesus' Birth
3. The Circumcision
4. The Prophecy of Simeon
5. The Flight into Egypt
6. The Return to Nazareth
7. The Losing of the Child Jesus in the Temple

The Seven Joys of St. Joseph

1. Told of the Incarnation
2. Angels Adore the Infant Jesus
3. Holy Name of Jesus
4. Effects of the Redemption
5. Overthrow of the Idols in Egypt
6. Life with Jesus and Mary
7. The finding of the Child Jesus in the Temple

Prayers in Honor of the Seven Joys and Sorrows of St. Joseph

1. O chaste Spouse of Mary most holy, glorious St. Joseph, great was the trouble and anguish of thy heart when thou wert minded to put away privately thine inviolate Spouse, yet thy joy was unspeakable when the surpassing mystery of the Incarnation was made know to thee by the Angel!

By this sorrow and this joy, we beseech thee to comfort our souls, both now and in the sorrows of our final hour, with the joy of a good life and a holy death after the pattern of thine own, in the arms of Jesus and Mary. (Recite the Our Father, Hail Mary, Glory Be.)

2. O most blessed Patriarch, glorious St. Joseph, who was chosen to be the foster father of the Word made flesh, thy sorrow at seeing the Child Jesus born in such poverty was suddenly changed into heavenly exultation when thou didst hear the angelic hymn and beheld the glories of that resplendent night.

By this sorrow and this joy, we implore thee to obtain for us the grace to pass over from life's pathway to hear the angelic songs of praise, and to rejoice in the shining splendor of celestial glory. (Recite the Our Father, Hail Mary, Glory Be.)

3. O glorious St. Joseph, thou faithfully obeyed the law of God, and thy heart was pierced at the sight of the Precious Blood that was shed by the Infant Savior during His Circumcision, but the Name of Jesus gave thee new life and filled thee with quiet joy.

By this sorrow and this joy, obtain for us the grace to be freed from all sin during life, and to die rejoicing, with the holy Name of Jesus in our hearts and on our lips. (Recite the Our Father, Hail Mary, Glory Be.)

4. O most faithful Saint who shared the mysteries of our Redemption, glorious St. Joseph, the prophecy of Simeon regarding the suffering of Jesus and Mary caused thee to shudder with mortal dread, but at the same time filled thee with a blessed joy for the salvation and glorious resurrection which, he foretold, would be attained by countless souls.

By this sorrow and this joy, obtain for us that we may be among the number of those who, through the merits of Jesus and the intercession of Mary the Virgin Mother, are predestined to a glorious resurrection. (Recite the Our Father, Hail Mary, Glory Be.)

5. O most watchful Guardian of the Incarnate Son of God, glorious St. Joseph, what toil was thine in supporting and waiting upon the Son of the most high God, especially in the flight into Egypt! Yet at the same time, how thou didst rejoice to have always near you God Himself, and to see the idols of the Egyptians fall prostrate to the ground before Him.

By this sorrow and this joy, obtain for us the grace of keeping ourselves in safety from the infernal tyrant, especially by flight from dangerous occasions; may every idol of earthly affection fall from our hearts; may we be wholly employed in serving Jesus and Mary, and for them alone may we live and happily die. (Recite the Our Father, Hail Mary, Glory Be.)

6. O glorious St. Joseph, thou didst marvel to see the King of Heaven obedient to thy commands, but thy consolation in bringing Jesus out of the land of Egypt was troubled by thy fear of Archelaus; nevertheless, being assured by the Angel, thou dwelt in gladness at Nazareth with Jesus and Mary.

By this sorrow and this joy, obtain for us that our hearts may be delivered from harmful fears, so that we may rejoice in peace of conscience and may live in safety with Jesus and Mary and may, like thee, die in their company. (Recite the Our Father, Hail Mary, Glory Be.)

7. O glorious St. Joseph, pattern of all holiness, when thou didst lose, through no fault of thine own, the Child Jesus, thou sought Him sorrowing for the space of three days, until with great joy thou didst find Him again in the Temple, sitting in the middle of the doctors.

By this sorrow and this joy, we supplicate thee, with our hearts upon our lips, to keep us from ever having the misfortune to lose Jesus through mortal sin; but if this supreme misfortune should befall us, grant that we may seek Him with unceasing sorrow until we find Him again, ready to show us His great mercy, especially at the hour of death; so that we may pass over to enjoy His presence in Heaven; and there, in company with thee, may we sing the praises of His Divine Mercy forever. (Recite the Our Father, Hail Mary, Glory Be.)

Antiphon. And Jesus Himself was beginning about the age of thirty years, being (as it was supposed) the Son of Joseph.

V. Pray for us, O holy Joseph,

R. *That we may be made worthy of the promises of Christ.*

Let us pray:

O God, who in Thine ineffable Providence didst vouchsafe to choose Blessed Joseph to be the spouse of Thy most holy Mother, grant, we beseech Thee, that he whom we venerate as our protector on earth may be our intercessor in Heaven. Amen.

Prayer

Pray for us, then, O great Saint Joseph, and by thy love for Jesus and Mary, and by their love for thee, obtain for us the supreme happiness of living and dying in the love of Jesus and Mary. Amen.

Traditional Memorare to St. Joseph

Remember, O most chaste spouse of the Virgin Mary, that never was it known that anyone who implored your help or sought your intercession was left unaided. Full of confidence in your power, I fly unto you and beg your protection. Despise not, O Foster Father of the Redeemer, my humble supplication, but in your bounty, hear and answer me. Amen.

St. Faustina's Memorare to St. Joseph

Saint Faustina wrote in her *Diary*:

> Saint Joseph urged me to have a constant devotion to him. He himself told me to recite every day three prayers [the Our Father, Hail Mary, and Glory Be], and the Memorare once every day. He looked at me with great kindness and gave me to know how much he is supporting this work [of mercy]. He has promised me his special help and protection. I recite the requested prayers every day and feel his special protection (1203).

The Memorare is the prayer to St. Joseph that St. Faustina's religious community recited daily:

> Remember, O most pure spouse of Mary, and my dearly beloved guardian, St. Joseph, that never was it known that anyone who invoked your care and requested your help was left without consolation.
>
> Inspired with this confidence, I come to you and with all the ardor of my spirit I commend myself to you. Do not reject my prayer, O Foster Father of the Savior, but graciously receive and answer it. Amen.

Other Prayers to St. Joseph

Prayer to St. Joseph

Hail, Joseph, image of God the Father.
Hail, Joseph, foster-father to God the Son.
Hail, Joseph, temple of God the Holy Spirit.

Hail, Joseph, beloved of the Holy Trinity!
Hail, Joseph, faithful servant of the plan of Redemption.
Hail, Joseph, worthy husband of the Virgin Mary.
Hail, Joseph, father to all the Christian faithful.

Hail, Joseph, guardian of God's people!

Hail, Joseph, lover of poverty and simplicity.
Hail, Joseph, example of meekness and holy patience.
Hail, Joseph, mirror of humility and faithfulness.

Hail, Joseph, teacher of the virtues!

Hail, Joseph, man of faith and virtue.
Blessed are you among all men.

Many longed to see what you saw,
And never saw it!
Many longed to hear what you heard,
And never heard it!

Hail, Joseph, you held the Word made flesh!
Hail, Joseph, you trusted in God's plan!
Hail, Joseph, who placed himself at God's service!

Blessed be the Father, who chose you.
Blessed be the Son, who loved you.
Blessed be the Holy Spirit, who sanctified you.

And blessed may we be
Who invoke your intercession,
And who, by the help of your prayers,
Want to love and serve God as you did. Amen.

Prayer to St. Joseph for Assistance

O glorious St. Joseph, you were chosen by God to be the foster father of Jesus, the most pure spouse of Mary ever Virgin, and the head of the holy family. You have been chosen by Christ's Vicar as the heavenly patron and protector of the Church founded by Christ. Therefore it is with great confidence that I implore your powerful assistance for the whole Church on earth. Protect in a special manner, with true fatherly love, the Pope and all bishops and priests in communion with the See of Peter. Be the protector of all who labor for souls amid the trials and tribulations of this life, and grant that all peoples of the world may follow Christ and the Church He founded.

Dear St. Joseph, accept the offering of myself which I now make to you. I dedicate myself to your service, that you may ever be my father, my protector, and my guide in the way of salvation. Obtain for me great purity of heart and a fervent love for the spiritual life. May all my actions, after your example, be directed to the greater glory of God, in union with the divine Heart of Jesus, the Immaculate Heart of Mary, and your own paternal heart.

Finally, pray for me that I may share in the peace and joy of your holy death. Amen.

Prayer to St. Joseph for Protection

Oh, St. Joseph,
whose protection is so great, so prompt, so strong
before the throne of God,
I place in you all my interests and desires.
Oh, St. Joseph,
do assist me by your powerful intercession,
and obtain for me from your Divine Son
all spiritual blessings through Jesus Christ, our Lord.
So that, having engaged here below your heavenly power,
I may offer my thanksgiving and homage to the most
Loving of Fathers.
Oh, St. Joseph,
I never weary contemplating you and Jesus asleep in
      your arms;
I dare not approach while He reposes near your heart.
Press Him in my name and kiss His fine Head for me and
Ask Him to return the Kiss when I draw my dying breath.
Saint Joseph, Patron of departed souls — pray for me.
Amen.

The Chaplet of St. Joseph

This chaplet is divided into 15 groups of four beads consisting of one white and three purple beads. The white beads symbolize St. Joseph's purity, and the purple, his saintly piety. A mystery of the Rosary is considered on each white bead and two "Hail Mary's" are said. On the purple beads, say "Praised and blessed be Jesus, Mary, and Joseph."

The chaplet is ended with the following prayer:

V. Pray for us, O Holy St. Joseph.

R. *That we may be made worthy of the promises of Christ.*

Let us pray:

O God, who has predestined St. Joseph from all eternity for the service of Thine eternal Son and His blessed Mother, and made him worthy to be the spouse of this blessed Virgin and the foster-father of Thy Son: we beseech Thee, through all the services he has rendered to Jesus and Mary on earth, that Thou wouldst make us worthy of his intercession and grant us to enjoy the happiness of his company in heaven. Through Christ Our Lord. Amen.

Prayer to St. Joseph for the Unemployed

O St. Joseph, we pray to you for those who are out of work, for those who want to earn their living or support their families.

You who are the patron of workers, grant that unemployment may vanish from our ranks; that all those who are ready to work may put their strength and abilities in serving their fellowmen and earn a just salary.

You are the patron of families; do not let those who have children to support and raise lack the necessary means. Have pity on our brothers and sisters held down in unemployment and poverty because of sickness or social disorders. Help our political leaders and captains of industry find new and just solutions. May each and every one have the joy of contributing, according to his abilities, to the common prosperity by an honorable livelihood. Grant that we may all share together in the abundant goods God has given us and that we may help the underprivileged. Amen.

Prayer for the Church Militant: Petitions and Dedication to St. Joseph

O glorious St. Joseph, you were chosen by God to be the foster father of Jesus, the most pure spouse of Mary ever Virgin, and the head of the holy family. You have been chosen by Christ's Vicar as the heavenly patron and protector of the Church founded by Christ. Therefore it is with great confidence that I implore your powerful assistance for the whole Church on earth. Protect in a special manner, with true fatherly love, the Pope and all bishops and priests in communion with the See of Peter. Be the protector of all who labor for souls amid the trials and tribulations of this life, and grant that all peoples of the world may follow Christ and the Church He founded.

Dear St. Joseph, accept the offering of myself which I now make to you. I dedicate myself to your service, that you may ever be my father, my protector, and my guide in the way of salvation. Obtain for me great purity of heart and a fervent love for the spiritual life. May all my actions, after your example, be directed to the greater glory of God, in union with the divine Heart of Jesus, the Immaculate Heart of Mary, and your own paternal heart. Finally, pray for me that I may share in the peace and joy of your holy death. Amen.

A Worker's Prayer to St. Joseph

Glorious St. Joseph, model of all those who are devoted to labor, obtain for me the grace to work in a spirit of penance for the expiation of my many sins; to work conscientiously, putting the call of duty above my inclinations; to work with gratitude and joy, considering it an honor to employ and develop, by means of labor, the gifts received from God; to work with order, peace, moderation, and patience, without ever recoiling before weariness or difficulties; to work, above all, with purity of intention, and with detachment from self, having always death before my eyes and the account which I must render of time lost, of talents wasted, of good omitted, of vain complacency in success, so fatal to the work of God. All for Jesus, all for Mary, all after your example, O Patriarch Joseph. Such shall be my watchword in life and in death. Amen.

Endnotes

Endnotes

Introduction

[1] For a brief introduction to the Mother of Jesus, see *Meet Your Mother*, Marian Press, 2014.

Chapter 1

[2] St. Teresa, *Autobiography of St. Teresa*, Ch. 6, n. 11.

[3] St. Francis de Sales, *The Spiritual Conferences*, English translation, Oates, 368.

[4] Blessed Pius IX, *Quemadmodum Deus*, December 8, 1870.

[5] Leo XIII, *Quamquam Pluries*, August 15, 1889.

[6] Pius XI, Papal Allocution, *L'Osservatore Romano*, March 19, 1938.

[7] St. John XXIII, Papal Allocution, March 19, 1961.

[8] St. John Paul II, *Redemptoris Custos*, n. 27.

[9] Pope Francis, May 2013 Liturgical Inclusion of the Name of St. Joseph into the Four Eucharistic Canons, *L'Osservatore Romano*, http://www.vatican.va/roman_curia/congregations/ccdds/documents/rc_con_ccdds_doc_20130501_san-giuseppe_en.html

[10] The Coat of Arms of Pope Francis, http://w2.vatican.va/content/francesco/en/elezione/stemma-papa-francesco.html

[11] April 30, 2014 *Vatican Insider*, www.vaticaninsider.com.

[12] October 13, 1917 Fatima apparition; cf. also July 13, 1917 Fatima apparition for revelation of the the promise of the "Triumph of the Immaculate Heart."

[13] October 1956 Messages of Our Lady of America, www.ourladyofamerica.org.

Chapter 2

[14] See Genesis 41:50.

[15] For one example of defense of the Assumption of St. Joseph, see St. Francis de Sales, *The Spiritual Conferences*, 19, 383.

[16] St. John XXIII, 1960, AAS 52, 455-456.

[17] For an excellent theological and devotional treatment of Old Testament patriarchs and types as models of fatherhood which are ultimately fulfilled in St. Joseph, see Devin Schadt, *Joseph's Way*, (distributed by Ignatius Press, 2013).

Chapter 3

[18] See Francis Filas, SJ, *Joseph: The Man Closest To Jesus*, (St. Paul Editions, Boston, 1962), p. 130. Note: This text is the definitive contemporary theological study on Josephite theology, written by the Jesuit theologian, Fr. Francis Filas. Several primary citations for our little work here have been re-cited from this much more comprehensive work.

[19] "Betrothal" in *Jewish Encyclopedia*, (Funk and Wagnalls, New York, 1916), 3. p. 130.

[20] George Foot Moore, *Judaism in the First Centuries of the Christian Era*, (Harvard University Press, Cambridge, 1927), 2. p. 121-122.

[21] Philo, *De leg. Spec.*, 3, 12, 72.

[22] St. Ambrose, *de instit. Virg.* 6, 41 (PL 16:316).

[23] St. Augustine, *de nup. et concup.* 1, 11, 12 (PL 44:421).

[24] Francis Filas, SJ, *St. Joseph after Vatican II*, (Alba House, New York, 1966), p. 142-143.

[25] Pope Benedict XVI, *Jesus of Nazareth: The Infancy Narratives*, (Image Books, New York, 2012), p. 39.

Chapter 4

[26] For a basic summary of Mary's Threefold Virginity, see Miravalle, *Meet Your Mother*, Chapter 3.

[27] *Protoevangelium of James*, as quoted in Filas, *The Man Closest to Christ*, p. 20.

[28] *Gospel of Pseudo-Matthew*, as quoted in Filas, *The Man Closest to Christ*, p. 26.

[29] Ibid.

[30] *History of Joseph the Carpenter*, op. cit.

[31] For example see Matthew 12:46, 13:55; Mark 3:31-32, 6:3; Luke 8:19-20; John 2:12, 7:3-5; Acts 1:14; 1 Corinthians 9:5; Galatians 1:19.

[32] Origen, *Commentary on Matthew*, 10:17; MPG 13, 875.

[33] Origen, *Homilia n Lucam*, 587; MPG 13, 1803.

[34] Jerome, *Adversus Helvidius*, MPL 19, 23, 203; see also *Commentary on Matthew*, 2, 12, 19; MPL 26, 89.

[35] Bede, *Homilia 5 in vigilia Nativitatis Domini*; MPL 94, 33.

[36] St. Peter Damian, *Opusculum 17, de caelibatus sacerdotum cap. 3*; MPL 145 384.

[37] For commentary on the subject, see Filas, *Joseph: The Man Closest To Jesus*, p. 83.

Chapter 5

[38] See Is 52, 53.

[39] See for example, reported messages of St. Joseph as found in the Messages of Our Lady of America, www.ourladyofamerica.org. N.B. These messages have been canonically evaluated and concluded to be already of the juridical status of an approved apparition by Cardinal (then Archbishop) Raymond Burke, *Letter to U.S. Conference of Catholic Bishops*, May 31, 2007. See also Chapter 9.

[40] Pope Benedict XVI, *Jesus of Nazareth: The Infancy Narratives*, p. 41.

[41] Emphasis added.

Chapter 6

[42] St. Epiphanius, *Adv. Haer.*, 51, 10 (MPG 41, 907).

[43] St. Augustine, *Sermo.* 51, Nos. 16, 20, 26, 30 (MPL 38, 342 ff.).

[44] St. Augustine, *Contra Faustum*, 3, 2, (Pl 42, 214).

[45] St. John Chrysostom, *Homily on Matthew*, 4, 6, (PG 57:47).

[46] St. Thomas Aquinas, *4 Sent.* 30.

[47] St. Thomas Aquinas, *Summa Theologiae* III, 28, a. 1 ad 1.

[48] Jacques-Benigne Bossuet, "First Panegyric upon St. Joseph," *Saint Joseph*, ed. and trans. By D. Attwater (P. J. Kenedy and Sons, N.Y., 1956).

[49] Pope Leo XIII, Mansi, 53, 581 as cited by Filas, *Joseph: The Man Closest to Christ*, p. 239.

Chapter 7

[50] See Filas, *Joseph: The Man Closest To Christ*, p. 477.

[51] Filas, *Joseph: The Man Closest to Christ*, p. 490-491.

[52] Filas, *Joseph: The Man Closest To Christ*, p. 483.

[53] St. Bernadine of Siena, *De S. Ioseph, Sponse B.V.M. sermo"*, Lessons of the Solemnity of St. Joseph.

[54] See Filas, *Joseph: The Man Closest to Christ*, pp. 139-140.

[55] John Gerson, *Considerations on St. Joseph*.

[56] Filas, *Joseph: The Man Closest to Christ*, p. 140.

[57] St. Teresa, *Autobiography of St. Teresa*, Ch. 6, n. 11.

[58] St. Teresa of Avila, *Autobiography*, Ch. 6.

[59] St. Teresa of Avila, *The Life*.

[60] St. Francis de Sales, *The Spiritual Conferences*, 38.

[61] Bossuet, "First Panegyric upon St. Joseph;" *Sermons sur Saint Joseph: Depositum custodi,* (Dominique Martin Morin, Poitiers, France, 1997); *Ovuerves Oratoires de Bossuet,* (Libraire Hachette, Paris, 1914).

Chapter 8

[62] Filas, *Joseph: The Man Closest To Christ*, p. 577.

[63] Pius IX, *Quemadmodum Deus*, Dec. 8, 1870.

[64] Ibid.

[65] *Hyperdulia* offered to Our Lady differs in nature and degree from the *Dulia* given the saints, while still being infinitely below the devotion of *Latria* due to God alone. See Miravalle, *Meet Your Mother*, Ch. 2.

[66] Pope Benedict XV, Motu Proprio, Bonum Sane, July 25, 1920.

[67] Ibid.

[68] Ibid.

[69] Pius XI, Encyclical Letter, *Divini Redemptoris*, March 19, 1937.

[70] Pius XI, *Allocution To Married Couples*, March 19, 1938.

[71] See Filas, *Joseph: The Man Closest to Christ*, p. 610-611.

[72] Pius XII, *Allocution to Christian Association of Italian Workers*, May 1, 1955, AAS 47, 402.

[73] St. John XXIII, Apostolic Letter, *Le Voci*, 19 March, 1961, L'osservatore Romano.

[74] St. John Paul II, Apostolic Exhortation, *Redemptoris Custos*, n. 31.

[75] St. John Paul II, Apostolic Exhortation, *Redemptoris Custos*, n. 32.

[76] *Decree on the Insertion of St. Joseph into Eucharistic Prayers II, III, IV*, Congregation of Divine Worship and the Discipline of the Sacraments. The decree was issued on May 1, 2013, Feast of St. Joseph the Worker, and made public on June 18, 2013.

[77] Pope Francis, July 5, 2014 Consecration of the Vatican City State to St. Michael the Archangel and St. Joseph, Vatican Information Service.

[78] Pope Francis, *Homily at Mass of Papal Inauguration*, March 19, 2014, Vatican Information Service.

Chapter 9

[79] Catherine Rynne, *Knock 1879-1979*, (Veritas Publishing, Dublin, 1979) p.11; see also Msgr. Arthur Calkins, *The Apparition of St. Joseph at Knock*, www.piercedhearts.org.

[80] As quoted in Jerome Palmer, *Our Lady Returns to Egypt*, (Culligan Publications, 1969), p. 42.

[81] May 31, 2007 Letter of Archbishop Raymond Burke to the United States Conference of Catholic Bishops, see www.ourladyofamerica.org. Why would the then-highest canonical authority under the Pope

state something so positive about a series of reported apparitions to a Ohio religious sister, Sr. Mary Ephrem (which began in the 1950s and continued, to some degree, until her death in 2000)?

The spiritual director of the visionary was the Archbishop of Cincinnati, Most. Rev. Paul Leibold. The Archbishop was instrumental in having these reported messages receive an *Imprimatur* from the Archdiocese. He further granted permission for a medal of Our Lady of America to be struck and he permitted the distribution of the messages — all of which constitute concrete signs and acts of official episcopal approval. Remember, it's the local bishop who has the first line of authority regarding the discernment of authenticity regarding any reported supernatural event within his diocese.

For these reasons and more, Cardinal Burke (when he was the highest canonical authority under the Pope) publicly stated his support of these reported apparitions as being already canonically approved based on the soundness of the message and the practice of the Archbishop during the time of the apparitions.

[82] To see the entire body of messages from Our Lady of America, go to www.ourladyofamerica.com. For several theological articles on Our Lady of America, go to www.Motherofallpeoples.com.

[83] For a new text on the subject, see Miravalle, *Who Dwells in You?*, (Gabriel Press, Hopedale, Ohio, 2014), www.motherofallpeoples.com.

[84] See Messages of Our Lady of America, 1956-58.

[85] Locution of St. Joseph, October, 1956, Messages of Our Lady of America, www.ourladsyofamerica.org.

[86] For example, St. John Paul II, *General Audience,* Jan. 30, 1982, *L'Osservatore Romano.*

[87] Message of St. Joseph, March 19, 1958, www.ourladyofamerica.org.

Chapter 10

[88] Congregation for the Doctrine of Faith, Approval of Personal Consecration to the Guardian Angel, *Opus Sanctorum Angelorum,* May 31, 2000.

PARISH EVANGELIZATION

Hearts Afire: Parish-based Programs from the
Marian Fathers of the Immaculate Conception (HAPP®)

STAGE ONE: The Two Hearts

PART 1: The Immaculate Heart

We begin our journey to the Immaculate Heart with the book *33 Days to Morning Glory* and its accompanying group-retreat program.

PART 2:
The Sacred Heart

Mary then leads us to the Sacred Heart, which begins the second part of Stage One with the book *Consoling the Heart of Jesus* and its accompanying group-retreat program.

STAGE TWO:
Wisdom and Works of Mercy

We begin Stage Two with *The 'One Thing' Is Three* and its accompanying group-study program, which gives group members a kind of crash course in Catholic theology. Stage Two concludes with a program for group works of mercy based on *'You Did It to Me.'*

STAGE THREE:
Keeping the Hearts Afire

At this point of ongoing formation, the Hearts Afire Team will recommend a wide range of further group parish renewal opportunities and more in-depth training that will suit the desires and needs of your group.

Hearts AFIRE

Parish-based Programs from the
Marian Fathers of the Immaculate Conception

1-866-767-3155
LighthouseCatholicMedia.org/HAPP